Career Enlighten

Ultimate Insider Strategies to Get and Enjoy Your Perfect Job, Income, and Fulfillment

YARDENA KRONGOLD

Copyright © 2022 Yardena Krongold.

All rights reserved. No part of this book may be used or reproduced by any means, graphic, electronic, or mechanical, including photocopying, recording, taping or by any information storage retrieval system without the written permission of the author except in the case of brief quotations embodied in critical articles and reviews.

Balboa Press books may be ordered through booksellers or by contacting:

Balboa Press
A Division of Hay House
1663 Liberty Drive
Bloomington, IN 47403
www.balboapress.com
844-682-1282

Because of the dynamic nature of the Internet, any web addresses or links contained in this book may have changed since publication and may no longer be valid. The views expressed in this work are solely those of the author and do not necessarily reflect the views of the publisher, and the publisher hereby disclaims any responsibility for them.

The author of this book does not dispense medical advice or prescribe the use of any technique as a form of treatment for physical, emotional, or medical problems without the advice of a physician, either directly or indirectly. The intent of the author is only to offer information of a general nature to help you in your quest for emotional and spiritual well-being. In the event you use any of the information in this book for yourself, which is your constitutional right, the author and the publisher assume no responsibility for your actions.

Any people depicted in stock imagery provided by Getty Images are models, and such images are being used for illustrative purposes only. Certain stock imagery © Getty Images.

Cover design: Vivian Krongold

Translation to Spanish: Vivian Krongold
Quotes selection: Lil Fernández and Yardena Krongold

Print information available on the last page.

ISBN: 979-8-7652-3656-7 (sc)
ISBN: 979-8-7652-3657-4 (hc)
ISBN: 979-8-7652-3669-7 (e)

Library of Congress Control Number: 2022921452

Balboa Press rev. date: 01/11/2023

Success Stories and Praise

Words from some of the top executives that Yardena Krongold and The Career Enlighten Academy have advised.

"Coaching for me has been extraordinary. You need to understand and do things differently; then, things change. Thanks to my results, my team and I became a success case study featured in Forbes US and HBR. It's a dream for me, and I never imagined these results…less in such a short time."

-Jorge Balestra
Global Head Machine Learning Operations
KraftHeinz

"She helped me assess and accelerate my career opportunities. Looking at different strengths and development areas, as well as exchanging ideas on specific top leadership situations—where you, as a leader, sometimes lack the chance to talk—was critical. Also, having an expert, neutral, and the best-prepared strategic view was a fantastic value for me—the best coach advice. I truly enjoyed and grew with the sessions! Thanks!"

-Patrick Eckert
Country President Brazil
Roche

"Yardena is an extraordinary professional with extensive experience in critical HR strategic areas —such as Talent Management, Strategic Staffing, and Organizational Development, among others—with broad strategic vision and business knowledge. I highly recommend her."

-Gabriela Garcia-Cortes
SVP and CHRO
PepsiCo

"Working with Yardena has been one of the best experiences in my career! In only three months of work, they secured a leadership position for me in a completely different industry with a high positive impact on my career. Achieving your dream job is a reality with her through impactful sessions and tools that assure impressive and fast results."

-Vanessa Flores-Shepard
Commercial Head
Ferrero ®

"I was promoted to a higher position and became an opinion leader in the global team at Big Pharma. I am grateful that our work together was critical to my next career step."

-Adriana Alvarez
Regional Medical and RA Lead LatAm
Bayer

"Serendipitously meeting Yardena on LinkedIn has been a blessing! With her help, I achieved the success I initially envisioned and got my first senior management role. She and her team exceed your expectations of executive career coaching as she has a unique mix of skills and has been successful in her career at very high levels. I strongly recommend their coaching to anyone seeking to take their life and career to the next level."

-Jorge Zepeda
Senior Sales Manager
BMW

"The organizational growth I got from Yardena's advice and strategies was astonishing. She helped me enhance my image and position inside my company, which opened new career path options beyond my dreams! They are undoubtedly experts in developing talent, creating tailored-made executive and business solutions, and enhancing corporate teams and culture. She has a powerful vision. A great experience to have the opportunity to be guided by her!"

-Oscar Monroy
Latin America PBR Lead and Country IT Head
Abbott

Praise from a worldwide authority on happiness and leadership

"Yardena Krongold has written a practical, evidence-based book that can help you realize your potential and positively impact your life and environment."

-Tal Ben-Shahar, Ph.D.
Author, Speaker, and Founder | Happiness Studies Academy & Potentialife[1]

---

[1] Ben-Shahar is an internationally renowned teacher, speaker, and author. He taught two of the most popular courses in Harvard's history: Positive Psychology and The Psychology of Leadership, with over 1,400 students per semester—approximately 20 percent of all Harvard graduates. *New York Times*-bestselling author, his books have been translated into more than 30 languages.

Praise from the most important global headhunter

"The most successful people are the ones that take action to develop themselves in all ways. They do not sit around waiting for their companies or bosses to prepare a career plan.

The biggest mistake is leaving your career in a company's hands. In this highly competitive market, you'll need the best expert advice and strategy to get where you want to be.

The only way is to reinvent yourself and take over your career, have emotional balance, and practice patience."[2]

-José Raúl Guerrero-Gantús
President of Mexico and CA | Korn Ferry

---

[2] Part of his speech during Yardena's first book, *Great Position, Paycheck & Purpose,* presentation (Publisher's note).

About the author

Yardena Krongold has spent over twenty-five years helping executives, leaders, and professionals achieve more successful, fulfilling, and lucrative jobs.

As HR Lead at KraftHeinz, Novartis, AT&T, Philip Morris, and Avon, she has an insider strategic view that accelerated her clients' results.

For years, she designed and implemented executive development strategies and programs that led thousands of people to grow to global, regional, and national critical positions in over seventeen countries.

She also created major state-of-the-art corporate universities focused on high-speed development programs for C-Suite executives, leaders, and senior managers in collaboration with Harvard Business School, Texas Tech, MIT, and Tec de Monterrey.

After practicing meditation and yoga for over three decades, she knows the path to get the best life balance and lifestyle, even in the most adverse and uncertain conditions.

She's a best-selling and prolific author of several books, including *Great Position, Paycheck & Purpose*. In this book, she shares many secrets to landing, nurturing, and growing high-end, meaningful, and fulfilling work in a tremendous teamwork environment.

To my coachees.
Of today, yesterday, and tomorrow. You realize that life has much more for you, and you want to use all your potential to create a unique and fulfilling life and career experience.
You are my inspiration!

To Vivian.
With her smile, curious green-blue gaze, human vision, and juvenile wisdom, she fills my days with joy, challenges, growth, and profound love. I treasure all your extraordinary gifts in this book!

Contents

Part I. Your journey starts here 1

Part II. Find complete fulfillment 11
   1. You don't need to endure it any longer 15
   2. It's not only about money 20
   3. A secret to speed up your rise 24

Part III. Hit a higher level 29
   4. The Five-Step Methodology to a career and life worth living 35
   5. Your brain: your best ally for greatness 37
   6. Your signature talents: a distinctive passport to success 41
   7. Online Assessment: your executive talent compass 52
   8. Your exposure: beyond personal branding 53

Part IV. Powerful Positioning Strategies 57
   9. Self-appraisal: How effective is your positioning and
      career strategy? 61
  10. Your job-getting commercial: leverage your expertise 63
  11. Your résumé and social media: entice your future bosses 69
  12. Your interviews: win the job without sweating 76

Part V. Make more money 81
  13. Are you underpaid? 87
  14. The hidden truth 92
  15. Are you suffering from invisible executive syndrome? 93

Part VI. Become unstoppable 97
    16. The treasure map is in your mind 101
    17. Who owns your career? 103
    18. Get rid of the brain programming that blocks you 107
    19. Being smart is not everything: mute your inner saboteur 111

Part VII. Break free to love yourself and life fully 117
    20. When the "perfect job" is not enough 121
    21. Silent violence: the soul's murderer 133
    22. Empower your career and life dreams 138

References 141
Index 145

Part I

Your journey starts here

When you think you know all the answers, comes
the universe, and it changes all questions.

—Albert Espinosa

"What does it take to reach a point where I'm truly happy and fulfilled? To do a job I love, that excites me, and that uses my full potential? To reach the level I deserve, I'm ready for, and be paid for what am I actually worth? To feel alive and connected?"

Not long ago, a new client came to me with these questions. They were keeping her awake every night. Have you ever felt this way? You're not alone.[3]

A few days ago, I was being interviewed and recalled sitting in a meeting room in Basel, Switzerland, with the global executive talent development team of one of the top-three pharmaceutical companies worldwide. We discussed new strategies to implement worldwide to accelerate our talent pipeline to meet the highly demanding business needs, commercial speed, and the aggressive product pipeline the corporation had envisioned for the next five years.

I had achieved a highly desirable position that many people would have loved to have, but paradoxically, a part of me wasn't pleased. It shocked me when I realized it. It was a great place to be, yet this inner voice was yearning for something more. I had not listened to this deep, subtle calling for many years.

---

[3] I wrote this book thinking of you, to help you remove all the obstacles and challenges you face when you try to make out of your career, your job, and your life a completely fulfilling experience, worthy of being lived and easily enjoyed.
Here you'll find the way to answer these concerns and the tools and strategies you will need to make your dreams and goals finally alive. These are the secrets and techniques I share with my clients to help them quickly attain their perfect jobs with the ideal fits without all the effort it usually takes.
You may also like to visit my website, www.careerenlightenacademy.com, where you'll get more free resources and the advice you need to accelerate your pace and enjoy the destination and the journey. If you need urgent support, email me at talktoyardena@careerenlightenacademy.com and we'll be happy to help you.

In some ways, the great job, the brand-new car, the beautiful house, the fantastic daughter, and the family were not enough. How is it even possible?

Don't get me wrong. I struggled a lot for a long time to get everything I had. There were times when it wasn't easy or fun at all. Then why wasn't it making me happy?

The battle was supposed to be over. All those years, I'd tried to thrive in the corporate game and eliminate the competition, conflicts, and hidden agendas to get a better role. All the time, I saw others being promoted and hired for the jobs I longed for while I remained invisible even though I was ready and exceeded expectations. How frustrating it was for me.

I remember feeling devastated. The social pressure, my perfectionism disguised as "high standards," and seeing others living and enjoying what I wanted made me feel like a failure, wholly inadequate, impotent, and furious.

I was angry with myself, with companies, and with the world. Why wasn't I capable of achieving what I wanted and was working on getting? Why didn't people value and recognize my ideas? Why didn't companies fulfill their promises? Why didn't they see and honor my results, effort, and commitment?

What was I doing wrong? I had a rough time trying to pay my mortgage and buy the kinds of cars other colleagues were driving. I almost lost my house and my car on two different occasions. Living in an apartment far away from downtown, I had to spend more than three hours commuting daily in a giant megalopolis. Waking up at 5:00 a.m. for a late-night type of person like me was hell. Every day, I woke up cursing life. I stumbled to keep pace with my peers' executive lifestyles. Still, I didn't understand how easy it seemed for them to have great outfits, cars, vacations, houses, and even hobbies—things I could only dream about. It was depressing, but the worst part was that it was so discouraging that it made me doubt my capacity, my values, and myself.

My head seemed to run between hundreds of questions with no answers. Why is it that others are earning much more, even when my results are much better? How do I make them see and recognize me for everything I am and do? Why are people with less potential and experience in better jobs? Why are others getting the promotions, the roles, and the visibility I am eager to have?

I was sure that answering these questions would take me exactly to the place I wanted, to enjoy the best of the best. But I didn't make up my mind and decide to truly take action and change the game until an urgent situation hit me in the face.

How it happened and moved me to turn around everything is a funny yet scary story.

While working at the biggest tobacco company, a friend called me on a Sunday at 9:00 p.m. He had to see me as something urgent had arisen, and he was already driving over to my house. I heard the urgency in his voice and prepared for the worst. When he arrived, he said he knew from a good source that the company was looking for my replacement.

I felt the world falling on me. It was not possible! I saw my house and my car slip out of my hands. Four people and I opened this company subsidiary from scratch in an emergent market a year and a half ago. It was a business that, to that date, not only had more than 2,500 employees but HR's best practices and more than beneficial business results in every way (sales, market share, talent pipeline, as well as many other key performance indicators). What part of my contribution to getting there wasn't clear to the company?

Terrified, I decided to find another job foremost. For the next three months, I went to almost a hundred interviews. I used my launch time and was in a crazy rush trying to prevent a disaster!

I have vast experience in staffing and every aspect of the talent attraction process. Now I could see and experience this process from the outside as a candidate. It became an excellent training field; it gave me the insights to perfect the positioning tools needed to win any job I wanted. Of course, I didn't realize and take complete advantage of that immersion life schooling until years later.

In the end, they didn't let me go, and as I didn't find a pretty fantastic job, I decided to stay.

One day, a call reached my phone. It was one of the regional directors who had interviewed me on one of those sad gray days. I had changed many things since then, and as a result, I had a promotion within the company. When the call came through, I wasn't into it. I said my position was different, so I'd only be interested in a D-level job with a four-month bonus, a salary 40 percent above, and a premium company car. To my surprise, I heard him say, "Yes, that's why I'm calling you! You must come!" I couldn't believe my ears. We had had an interview one year before for another position, he had kept my business card, and when he had a higher job to offer me, he called me—and not only called me but hired me!

Even though it took me so long to understand what I had to change, learn, and gather to create the powerful techniques and tools necessary, it took me little to no time to implement those changes to start growing and stand out when I reached that C-suite office in Basel.

Yet, that annoying inner voice was there yelling at me, "This can't be everything in life." It seemed I had to face a second and more profound challenge—life had more fun awaiting me!

The truth is that I didn't feel complete.

At first, it was irritating. Then I started listening. What is this inner voice of mine asking me? Why do I still feel something is missing? I began to recognize my deep yearnings buried inside it. I wanted to break free. I did not want to be stuck in a golden cage! I wanted to own my time and career decisions and do something transcendent. I wanted to feel filled with energy and enthusiasm, to live new, exciting experiences, and to enjoy life fully.

As I listened more carefully, everything became more explicit. All those years of reading, researching, and struggling made me aware of the unnecessary struggles we sometimes live with. Most important was the need to overcome them with the proper approach and strategies—stopping all the frustration and suffering they bring.

This insight was the turning point to start helping people on a different scale with a broader scope. I decided to help others and share everything I knew with them to make their journeys faster, easier, and more pleasant. Mainly I wanted to help them achieve lives and careers they'd genuinely love and thoroughly enjoy.

I used to put all these techniques and strategies at one company's service, developing internal talent, launching corporate universities, and creating centers of excellence. However, this was too important to be used only for one company's benefit, even with more than 150,000 employees worldwide, and the gift had to expand further.

I had the potential to change many people's lives, not only one executive's career and life, but the careers and lives of thousands of people and everyone around them: their teams, their children, their families, and their friends. When we reach our highest potentials, we permit others to do so. It's not that they need our permission; they see us thrive, conquer our doubts and fears, overcome struggles with ease, and achieve new objectives without all the effort it usually takes. That's inspiring and healing! It's precious in a world trying to take us down in many ways.

My life's mission arouses my mind in a very natural way.

I had to help everyone pursue fulfilling lives worth living and rewarding jobs worth doing. I had to make all these state-of-the-art strategies and techniques—usually available to a handful of executives in the most significant companies—open to people trying to achieve these results. That became my life's mission.

After working with so many people for so many years, I can't help but feel profound joy and gratitude every time one of them opens a new door and perspective that leads that person to reach inner longings in his or her job and life.

Now, whenever I work with any of my clients—whether in private programs, teams, or groups—my mantra is to break new ground to grow, free the mind, and free the soul.

When I look back at everything I have accomplished, all the people I have helped achieve more joyous work and life experiences, I see the words of my beloved guru shining firmly in front of me. When you don't get what's here for you, you feel the world is slipping away from you. But worry will not bring the solution. Get down to work, and adopt this determination:

I will shake the world until I get what's meant for
me. I won't stop until it meets my needs!⁴

—Paramahansa Yogananda

---

[4] In the hundred years since the birth of Paramahansa Yogananda, this beloved spiritual master has come to be recognized as the father of yoga in the West and one of the preeminent spiritual figures of the twentieth century. His life and teachings bring major inspiration and light to people of all races, cultures, and creeds. According to the publisher, Self-Realization Fellowship, "*Autobiography of a Yogi* is at once an absorbing account of the singular search for Truth and a profound introduction to the whole science and philosophy of Yoga." Many great leaders have followed his teachings and path. Steve Jobs' last gift was a copy of this enlightening book handed out at his memorial service (Segall 2013). George Harrison also used to gift this book to his friends and people he met (Yoganda Site 2016).

Part II

Find complete fulfillment

I would rather not do it than do it and it not be fun.

—Harry Styles

You don't need to endure it any longer

I'm sitting on my deck enjoying the afternoon and the beautiful sea view and suddenly feeling deeply grateful for an enormous sense of freedom. What a different feeling it is from those Sundays when I thought I couldn't confront the upcoming week and Monday was coming upon me.

I know that sometimes Monday can be uphill, and I have lived it. I also know how difficult it can be to move to a situation that, instead of draining us, makes us feel in control, enthusiastic, recognized, and happy.

I remember those old days when it was hard for me to wake up and face reality. I tried to hold on to the weekend so it would never end. Obviously, that never happened, and I had to meet stressful, dull days at work doing something I didn't enjoy in a remarkably hostile environment.

If today you have a job that you love, that allows you to live up to your full potential, and gives you all the financial freedom, recognition, and life experiences you want, you are lucky as I am now. For that, I feel very grateful—for you and me.

Believe me, if you haven't gotten there yet, there is a way to do it.

Now you have the opportunity to change your future and your life. Take them on a beautiful journey to hit a place where you enjoy the job, career, and life experiences you want.

There are no coincidences. If you are reading this book, it may be because a part of you is restless and wants more. And, even though it may sound weird, I positively celebrate it!

After helping so many executives achieve their most ambitious goals, I've learned that the only way of having and making real a genuinely exciting career path is by taking perspective. This means first clearing our minds of the demands of our current worries and duties, whatever they may be, for a moment. Second, it involves bringing to consciousness the indispensable elements you need to keep moving forward in your career and shield them against any risks. Let's face it: any career that doesn't move forward gets stuck and eventually dies.

Take perspective to accelerate your career.

These pages are precisely about helping you take the view you need and giving you the most infallible tools. They will help you accelerate the achievement of your goals, whatever they may be!

I live in a world where anything is possible, and I want to invite you to get into it and play with me today.

Confession: My Working Addiction

Let me tell you why I believe anything is possible: I was a workaholic—ring a bell?

I lived 100 percent for my job. My days were full of stress, long meetings, routines, impatient bosses, and fatigue. I couldn't make time for anything else, not even eating—literally—much less think about hanging out with friends, meeting a nice guy, or having a family life. Though I had a great position that allowed me to live excellently, I used to yearn for a more exciting life filled with funny people, new experiences, and leisure time in the most beautiful places on earth.

I thought it was unfair that I worked so hard and delivered outstanding results, yet I couldn't find time and energy for other amusing, social, and outdoor activities.

Now, after an incredible journey, I live the life of my dreams. I have a beautiful daughter with whom I have built a significant deep relationship, live in a fantastic house in a magnificent place, and recently have found new dreams and profoundly meaningful life goals. I feel genuinely happy most days. I enjoy the benefits of having international recognition, a successful career that not only brings me great abundance but allows me to work on what I love, and nonetheless, I'm the absolute owner of my schedule. I even take vacations when I want, for as long as I decide.

But that's not it. Over the past decades, I've helped hundreds of executives reach their highest career and life goals. I've discovered that anything is possible.

Since I became involved in executive development and coaching, I've seen all my career goals and inner dreams come to life.

I'm telling you all this because I'm confident you can achieve this kind of success—and much more. I also know that there may be a part inside you asking,

Is it really possible to achieve a job that meets all my desires?

A few days ago, I posted on Instagram and Facebook about a very dark and painful episode in my life, which few people knew about—even family and close friends.[5]

---

[5] You can read about it in the last part of this book, under the section "Silent violence: the soul's murderer." If you live something similar to what I did, I intend that here you'll find the strength and tools to recover your freedom and your power. You deserve it!

Many people wrote me not only to be supportive and empathize with me but also to thank me in two different ways. Some thanked me for the help I gave them that was crucial to getting them out of critical situations in their careers or lives. Others shared with me the obstacles they're currently facing.

One of them wrote:

> Our work together helped me transform my life and work in ways I had never imagined. In addition to all the robust strategies tailored to the challenges I was struggling with, you gave me back my confidence and the strength to achieve my goals. And it all started when you asked me, "How long are you going to endure it?"

That's the first question I'd like you to ask yourself.

If you are in a condition that does not fulfill you 100 percent in your job or any other aspect of your life,[6] I'd like you to ask yourself these five enlightening questions.

It doesn't have to be extreme or severe; sometimes, even small discontents bring massive long-term frustrations. Frankly, it's easier to identify harsh and radical situations than veiled ones. So, identify any discomfort you may feel deep down—anything that might come up is okay.

---

[6] I was in a highly toxic relationship that took me years to leave because I did not want to face reality. I kept telling myself a "happy story," and feared to "overcomplicate" my life even more. The main question you want to ask yourself is *How am I contributing, feeding, and creating this situation for myself?*

Five Enlightening Questions

Try to answer these questions thoroughly. You may want to sit in a nice quiet place and let your mind look into your current reality and the new future you'll start creating for yourself. Keep in mind that anything is possible. It doesn't matter if you don't know how to achieve it—that's what we're here for.

1. What is the most challenging part of what I am living now?

2. Do I want this to be my life, or do I want to move on to something better?

3. What would I have to change to feel satisfied, recognized, and more energized?

4. Am I in the exact place I want to be?

5. Where do I truly want to be?

If there's a part of you that wonders if it's possible, don't worry. It is the delusion trying to keep you where you don't want to be.

The truth is that everything is attainable. Today some people are living the life you want, enjoying the level and position you want, and working in an environment like the one you would like, surrounded by people who value and recognize them, with time and energy to do what they want the most.

It's not only about money

"It's not just about the money," he said. "It's about the place I deserve."

These were the words of one of my coachees. He had just received the offer for a magnificent promotion he reached after a couple of months of our work together. He wanted to negotiate an extra raise on the company's job offer, so we got to work.

In the end, he got a regional head role to manage over twelve countries with a 40 percent increase in his salary and overall executive package. This new job was the highest position he had ever held in his career and included a second area that wasn't entirely of his expertise: medical.

His success filled me with joy, although I was not surprised. I was sure he'd make it, but he wasn't. The path had been challenging. We had to work hard on diverse topics, from his confidence and beliefs to his political savviness and ability to convey his value to the organization to strengthen his positioning. It all paid off, and he got the position and the salary he deserved.

Something I love about my job is when my clients discover in awe that they achieved what they thought was out of their league and realize the enormous return on investment they had on their work with me. In only one year, he'll get fifty-seven times what he invested; for every dollar invested in his coaching program with me, he'll get $57. Imagine if you multiply that figure by the time remaining in his career with this new level; he'll get a return on investment (ROI) of 570 percent in ten years, 855 percent in fifteen, and 1,140 percent in twenty. What banking investment instrument gives you even a percentage of this gain? The best investment you can make is getting yourself ready with the tools, strategies, skills, and confidence you need to achieve great professional and financial goals.

While writing this, I wonder how you feel about these numbers. Is there a little voice within you that tells you it's not possible? Or it's not for you? Or will it be a heavier weight to have that kind of growth?

Yes, it sounds familiar. We all have an ambivalent relationship with money. On the one hand, having money is super desirable, and we all want more—fiercely. At the same time, we fear having more. We fear it will negatively affect us somehow. What if people stop loving us for what we are? What if we end up lonely and devastated as all those millionaires?

After all, conventional "wisdom" suggests that "money can't buy you happiness"—or love, as The Beatles said. Don't get me wrong—I'm a raving fan of The Beatles. I'm sure that "the best things in life are free" and "love is the answer," but that doesn't mean we have to give up on our wealth. Actually, money is just another expression of energy and all-prevailing love. We'll go into that later.

We live on such an abundant and generous planet that shows us we deserve better. In the end, we get what we think we deserve. And people earn precisely what they expect to make.

That's why it is fundamental to work with our money beliefs and emotions if we're to claim our birthright: abundance. I want you to dynamite all the sayings on money: how difficult it is to make, how easy it is to lose it, and how blessed those are who don't need it or save it, "spending is quick, earning is slow," and "a small leak will sink a big ship." I know this might be challenging because of how our brains are wired.[7] Email us at hello@careerenlightenacademy.com if you find it especially hard, and we'll share some more resources to help you.

Although the list of sayings is endless, new research shows differences. Researchers Matthew Killingsworth at the University of Pennsylvania and Nobel prize winners Daniel Kahneman and Angus Deaton found in different studies that higher levels of wealth are consistently associated with greater well-being. Killingsworth used two measures of well-being (happiness in general and life satisfaction), while Kahneman and Deaton focused on life evaluation and emotional well-being.

Killingsworth and Daniel Gilbert of Harvard University found other interesting facts. On one hand, "a wandering mind is an unhappy mind," and on the other, that freedom to innovate, create, and make yourself into something also makes you happier. This should not surprise us if we know about other studies that show that nine out of ten people are willing to earn less money to do more meaningful work (Achor, Reece, Rosen Kellerman, and Robichaux 2018). This significant number is interesting; it offers a worldwide beautiful newborn tendency we want to nurture, but is it indispensable to choose? Or may we learn to create a better and richer scenario for ourselves?

Their subsequent finding is shocking.

> As soon as people reach the necessary level of income that makes them feel comfortable, they begin to criticize the ambitions of those attempting to rise up. You won't hear "money isn't everything" as much in the Czech Republic, Mexico, or Bangladesh as you will in France, the United States, or Japan. (Achor et al. 2018)

We are not just talking about money, which, as we stated, is essential. We are talking about the life experiences you would like to have and how you want

---

[7] To understand how your brain works and why our beliefs are so difficult to change, you may think of 1999's cult film *The Matrix*, where humanity is trapped inside a simulated reality. The illusion enslaving humanity is a world—the matrix—feeding artificial signals to people's brains. In the same way those men and women were unable to go beyond their thoughts, our brains cling to and defend toxic and limiting beliefs as if they were the ultimate reality. To learn more, signup at www.careerenlightenacademy.com/brainseries.

to take advantage of this moment in which humanity is discovering new horizons and priorities. Half of the population is wondering, *Is this all there is? Or are there other things that could also be interesting and important to me? What shape do I want my life and career to take from here?*

These life and career-transforming goals may take as many forms as there are people in the world.

For one of my coachees, it meant enjoying an ex-pat assignment, with all its privileges, while living in front of Central Park. For another, it was starting her own sales force excellence business and selling their services to European companies. For another, it involved changing paths from the fourth consumer packaged goods company to joining as chief financial officer at the largest non-profit organization focused on helping women worldwide, all while keeping her status and salary.

What would it mean for you? What would it be like to get to the place you deserve? What do you see there? Maybe you're already in a position you like and want to take things further? What would upgrade your experience and make it even more enjoyable? Where do you want to go from here?

It's not just about the money, as my coachee said. It's about your life and the career you deserve.

A secret to speed up your rise

After over twenty-five years of designing and using the most powerful state-of-the-art strategies to help executives achieve and speed up their professional, financial and personal goals, I am excited to share them with you in this growth, reflection, and learning space.

If you are reading this, it's most likely that you are interested in reaching new goals in your career. I love that because it is my specialty.

Let's dive into what you want to achieve. These are some of the primary goals most people pursue, but I'd like you to think about your own life and job.[8]

An exciting new, more meaningful, and rewarding job
A higher and more lucrative role
A more comfortable financial position and a better lifestyle
Improved work-life balance to enjoy other important things
A change in career paths to something more enticing

---

[8] You may go back to the five enlightening questions in Chapter 1. I'm sure you'll find them very useful.

Getting back in business
Enjoying better conditions in a current job
Personal growth: finding the right person, improving life, and so on
Acquiring more confidence, energy, and peace of mind
Starting a new successful side business

You probably found that some point matches your goals and dreams; that's great—you're alive! Don't let anyone tell you that you can't achieve everything you want.

It's not only possible but inevitable with the right tools you'll find here with me. I'm determined to give you every technique and strategy to help you get there the easiest and fastest way.

Others may have found that they're not that clear about what you want. It's okay too, and there are tools to help you clarify your direction.

One way or another, *you are in the perfect place.*

To start, I would like to share one of the critical facts of success that helped me achieve where I am now and that I use with my clients to help them reach their highest goals. Of all the different things I have tried since I discovered these techniques, this is the one that surprised me the most.

On those dark days when I was trying to reach higher positions and grow within the corporate business without the immediate success I wanted, I used to feel frustrated.

Don't get me wrong; I already had an attractive career, full of everything I would have wanted, nevertheless, for a second, I could sometimes see something bigger and brighter for me. In front of me, a new path appeared that seemed more attractive than everything I had achieved so far. Perhaps I had read or heard something that inspired me or made me see my top talents and potential in a different way.

The fact is that suddenly I found myself full of enthusiasm to explore that new perspective, whether it was a new and more fulfilling job, a more attractive company, or a new role in my dream country. I could almost see myself achieving it.

Practically I could hear the comments around me, my family being proud of me, my daughter looking up at me with respect and admiration. What a feeling!

I truly wanted to be there and felt motivated to do whatever was necessary to achieve it. I wanted to tell the world. The first thing to do was talk about my plans with my colleagues, friends, and family, with anyone who could give me a suggestion and with whom I could share my vision and enthusiasm.

What a big mistake!

Then, it would happen: that impetus diluted and vanished without me realizing or doing anything to avoid it. My mind simply moved somewhere else, focused on other stuff—day-to-day life, results, work priorities, meetings, anything—and I seemed to forget my resolution to take action to achieve my new path.

Yes, it was baffling and upsetting.

You may be going through this. You want to move toward your objective, days go by, and it seems there is something in your way: you can't find the time, the energy, or the best strategy to implement and get results.

In my experience, nothing changed until I started to do something completely different. I began to be silent and stopped talking about what I wanted to do, stopped asking for opinions and ideas.

Now instead of talking about it, I was doing it.

How to Take Smart Action

Finally, I was able to make time and invest energy; in fact, I even found the support I needed from two coaches, first in Germany and then in the United States (Daniel and Christian, thank you guys—you both rock!). They arrived just at the right moment.

How?
What changed?
What did I do differently?

Take note: this is a habit I have always recommended that my clients nurture ever since.

Instead of running to inspire others with my plans (or sometimes searching for their approval or trying to convince them), I kept my vision only in my mind. I hid it like it was an art piece, an artist's secret that I didn't want anyone to see.

Silence Became My Secret Weapon

Later I found out why and how it works.

Peter Gollwitzer of New York University has been studying for decades how announcing your plans to others satisfies your self-identity just enough that you're less motivated to do the hard work needed. (Gollwitzer 2009).

We all love to receive compliments from others and to be seen as important and admirable people. When sharing our intentions with our peers, we start to enjoy the rewards and reputation we are looking for.

The simple fact of sharing our ideas about reaching the level, the position, and the job we dreamed of makes us feel a fake satisfaction that weakens our capacity to make decisions and enact them.

We become *legends* in our minds, and tales don't get their hands dirty with hard work.

The Worst Part

In my extensive experience working with people, I have discovered that we can find an infinite number of haters and blockers when talking about our goals. It sounds hard to believe, right?

However, if we take a closer look at these haters and blockers, sometimes we can see emotional reactions in them that tie us to our current situations, doubts, and fears; sometimes we even see envy. Distracting and convincing voices are looking to make us stay where we are. It's not because our friends don't appreciate us or they have malicious intentions. Most times, it's for their personal reasons, but that's a topic for another day.

You most likely have heard people say about someone, "Poor thing. She lost her job, and it's been months!" These voices work against our efforts to thrive as they collaborate with our toxic emotions, such as self-pity.

Beyond the difficulties of today's complex and competitive job market, when we face this kind of reaction we're likely up against other types of forces we do not even realize exist.

That's when expert support and objective assessment take on leading roles.

From now on, you know the deal. If you really want to achieve it, shhhhh, keep it a secret. It is your secret weapon.

Part III

Hit a higher level

I know, on the contrary, what I no longer want to be, where I no longer go.

—Katherine Pancol

We have incredible brains, but one of their boundaries is imagination, and we cannot go to a place we haven't imagined.

It's easier to know what we don't want, and it's a natural process of life. We live some experience and decide we didn't like it and don't want to go through it again. If we're paying enough attention, we may figure it out. What might be tremendously hard is knowing what we want.

When my coachees first come to me, I like to make a diagnosis of their careers to design a tailored-made program to help them speed up their goals.

When talking about what we'd like in our lives and careers, most of us only see generalities of little use to guide our brains, actions, and strategies in the right direction. We need to dig deep into what we want if we're to make it actually happen.

You want to achieve a meaningful and completely fulfilling job and life. You want a job and a life that give you all the financial freedom, inspiring leadership, creative opportunities, inclusive and rewarding culture, teamwork environment, attractive challenges, and everything that matters to you and honors who you are. To do that, you need to start thinking about and designing your new life.

In this chapter, I'll share meaningful and valuable insights on every step you need to take to start moving faster toward your goals. You may also want to use my newly released eBook, *5 Easy Steps To Speed Up Your Career*; it's a guide to discovering more about your unique path. You can download it here: bit.ly/5stepsspeedup.

The Five-Step Methodology
To a career and life worth living

Here is the five-step methodology I've designed and used to position over 5,750 executives and people in their perfect jobs with the ideal fits and lives.

1. Career Path and Strategy

    a. Ensure short and long-term goals.
    b. Routes, highways, and shortcuts.
    c. Focused brain.

2. Powerful Positioning System

    a. Unbeatable résumé. Maximize value and competitive advantage.
    b. Signature talents. Convey the whole experience and potential.
    c. Appealing LinkedIn profile. Generate real opportunities.
    d. Assertive interviews that portray calmness. Avoid costly mistakes. Handle objections and challenging questions. Connect to create bonding and relevance.

3. **Salary and Career Negotiations**

    a. Effectively negotiate job offers, salary proposals, conditions, benefits, promotions, increases, and career moves.

4. **Networking and Stakeholder Engagement**

    a. Effective and extensive networking.
    b. Expand networking to new critical hiring managers and decision-makers.

5. **Mindset, Emotional Intelligence, and Inner Growth**

    a. Strengthen mindset. Face difficult moments. Achieve confidence and peace of mind. Eliminate limiting beliefs, toxic thoughts, and habits.

Your brain:
Your best ally for greatness

Not long ago, I had a hard time doing things I wanted to do in my life.

I literally couldn't find a way to get my mind to accept the idea of exercising physically. I tried to schedule it, studied the advantages, bought attractive outfits, and subscribed to a fantastic sports club. Well, I did everything except for the main thing. My mind refused to accept the matter.

Until recently, it was not easy for me to select the most potent ideas for my masterclasses and workshops. My mind had a vast universe of great ideas and topics, and although, in the end, I succeeded, it used to take me a long time and effort to find the way.

I feel very excited and privileged to share these discoveries with you. Thank you, Ima, for letting me in on these life-changing findings.

Make Your Brain Work for You

Thanks to advanced diagnostic methods that scan the brain and display images in real-time, a new universe of findings and knowledge about our brain activity is available today. Researchers explore every day in more detail how the brain is wired and how its circuits are activated.

We've learned that the brain is constantly growing and changing. It's no longer true that it's immovable, that brain cells (neurons) degenerate but can't regenerate and multiply.

They have shown us that our brains are the most potent and malleable organisms on earth.

Brain Plasticity

Your brain can grow in the most important thing: its structure. Not only are more neurons generated continuously, but the number of connections and wiring increases all the time.

Imagine that brain circuits are like the wiring in a large building and that the neural connections that enable all of your activity—your thoughts, ideas, emotions, and actions—are the contacts on the walls. Good.

It is as if you not only placed more contacts in that building to connect more things but also placed more cables to multiply the electrical circuit.

What good is it to you to know that the brain has a configuration that constantly changes?

Why would you want to know that you have between eighty-six and one hundred billion neurons and can have up to 15,000 connections with other neurons via synapses? That is over 1000 trillion synaptic connections. The number of your brain connections is larger than the sum of galaxies in the whole universe[9] and the Milky Way stars.[10]

Moreover, you've probably read some of this data somewhere, but how can it serve you in your life? How could you use it to your advantage?

---

[9] The Hubble Space Telescope has discovered about 100 billion galaxies in the universe.
[10] Astronomers estimate there are about 100 thousand million stars in the Milky Way alone.

Because neuroplasticity is fed and grows when you acquire new skills, your brain expands, and certain areas grow stronger. You'll find this is gold if you want to

- ✓ Develop new skills in the blink of an eye to become an expert in any field and a well-rounded, attractive executive or professional;
- ✓ Get to the place where the results flow quickly and effortlessly; or
- ✓ Stop struggling and suffering with things that don't come naturally to you, like public speaking, senior-level executive presentations, influencing and persuading your peers, communicating negative news to your team, or any other activities.

Strengthen Your Brain for Fast Results

Scientists have found that brain activity is the same whether you're doing any action or just imagining yourself performing it.

For instance, when you play the piano, certain areas of your brain light up with particular intensity, showing the brain's activity. Now, when you imagine and move your fingers as if you were playing the piano, the same areas light up with the same intensity.

After some weeks of practicing the exercise in the real physical world, your brain will show growth in the areas involved. The incredible thing is that if you practice only in your mind, imagining moving your fingers in the same routine, the same regions will show growth almost to the same degree.

Just Imagine

Now you can see the power this knowledge gives you.

Imagine doing it if you want to be good at selling your ideas to the executive committee, the CEO, or any audience. Imagine you're addressing them, owning your speech, and conveying what you want, then practice as if you were before them.

If you want to be good at public speaking, start visualizing yourself in front of an audience and think about improving your posture and voice modulation. Think about the language you'll use to emphasize your ideas; imagine yourself fearlessly talking, confident in your ability.

Then magical things will happen in your brain, and you will exercise the areas needed to perform this precise action smoothly and efficiently. Thus, your brain will go beyond just getting used to the idea and will help you achieve the result you want.

Sounds good? Magnificent! To have the most remarkable result, you will need to apply this magical technique to the skills and activities (your signature talents) that will take you to the next level of success in your career. With them, you'll find out that your path is unique.

Your signature talents:
A distinctive passport to success

I'm aware that many of you want to know more about using all the most recent neuroscience discoveries to accelerate your pace toward achieving your ideal job, finances, and lifestyle. It's especially true if you've been struggling or just not moving as fast and accurately as you'd like. You may be tired of seeing everyone around you wearing themselves out to achieve their own or some growing more quickly than you have done so far.

Well, I want to tell you that these strategies and techniques are not only the easiest and fastest ways to achieve them but ones you'll enjoy the most and have lots of fun with.

Even so, the percentage of executives who deeply understand and exploit their talents in their full depth is meager.

Let's start by defining what I mean by signature talents. They go far beyond our executive skills, although they might include them. If we focus our scope on our skills, as we do most of the time, there may or may not be a differentiator from the rest of the candidates. We're losing the opportunity to make a statement and a differentiated value proposition: the results we can deliver and they won't find from any other executive.

Talents are those areas and topics where you can make a substantial difference to your future bosses' results which they are eager to get.

Identifying these talents and building a bridge—verbal, visual, and conceptual—to the results we will create for our future bosses is at the core of a powerful positioning strategy and one of the most complex challenges for any executive.

It's something I work on with my clients regularly, as it feeds their résumés, LinkedIn profiles, and other marketing materials. It also nurtures how they look at their experiences, potential, and ability to upgrade their positioning and communicate them most appealingly and accurately.

Why Is It So Hard to Unveil Them?

As soon as we try to discover our talents, all kinds of doubts, thoughts, and voices arise in our heads, making it difficult to see objectively. It seems that these talents are commonplace. In fact, sometimes we even feel more comfortable copying what we have seen others do, which destroys any chance we might have had of having a high-impact application.

Discovering your talents and creating a positioning strategy requires you to get out of yourself and your perspective and achieve a comprehensive vision of your work and yourself. The point is that it is very difficult, or almost impossible, to transmit the added value you will give when chosen for a position if you do not know and value your talents.

Here's a guide to start unveiling them.

Blow Your Mind with Pleasure

Have you ever been doing something and feel that only a few minutes have passed when in fact hours have passed? Have you learned something very quickly and it seemed simple and fun while others were racking their brains trying to understand it?

That's the *place* where everything flows out of you without any effort, and that's where we want to get to. The big question is how to do that.

The answer lies in discovering and shining your signature talents. The secret lies in how to do it.

We live in societies and companies emphasizing our shortcomings and weaknesses. We may call them opportunities or development areas, yet most of our feedback is about our flaws. At school, at work, and at home, people seem to be experts on everything we need to improve.

Get Rid of Your Shortcomings and Weaknesses

Contrary to what we have been taught, the only way to stand out and flow when we do something is to develop and work from our talents. Recent research has found that the path to levels of excellence is to nurture what comes naturally to us with ease and fun; those are your talents. They can be as varied as there are people in the world.

Don't think there is a list or dictionary of talents from which you must select your own, and voilá. It's going to take a bit more than that. The bad news is that the language to describe talents is still being created. It will be a gigantic task to capture the subtle differences to understand someone's singular talents deeply.

The good news is that you can discover them within you. Let's start exploring yours.

Your Talents Are What Make You Unique

Your talents make you unique and set you apart from the rest of the people in the world. Each one of the eight billion people is special. What you have to give to the world is unique; if you don't provide it, the world will lose it.

Don't think I'm telling you this to make you feel good. No, I'm telling you because it's true. Your talent gives your stamp to your work and everything you do in your life.

By talent, I don't mean a description like the ones we usually find in regular CV summaries or tests like Myers-Briggs. They might give you good hints if you do a good analysis. Still, you'll stay in the gray zone if you don't dig any further. They say very little about your true self. Most importantly, they won't make you stand out from the rest, or introduce your strength and uniqueness as a high-flying executive in a potent way.

Your signature talents are inherent to who you are; they are impressed in your DNA. Your brain is designed and wired to provide great enjoyment and results in potent ways when you work and create from them.

Don't be afraid to dig into your expertise and potential to find the traces that will lead you to discover them.

You may find them in your reactions, ways of being, strengths, and, sometimes, even traits that might seem negative but can be talents if applied productively. Stubbornness, for example, might be a talent that a chief marketing officer may need to stay at the top of his or her game despite enormous resistance. Obviously, that stubbornness will need to be polished and renamed to be presented as a positive trait.

On the other hand, it's also essential to know that maybe your talents are not strengths yet. To turn them into strengths, you may need to uncover, name, and nurture skills, habits, and patterns of thought you won't even see today. Then, they will become areas of excellence.

Do you remember how to let your brain work for you? Check it out.

Genius at Work

Here's how to discover and dig deeper into your talents, then use them to get the job, the paycheck, and the enjoyment you're looking for.

Let's find some data.

1. Review your last two or three performance reviews, your 360 degree survey, the results of your area's latest engagement survey, your

client satisfaction survey, or any other instrument that measures how others perceive you.

If you don't have any of those, or want to improve your findings, you can ask your colleagues for feedback. Ask your peers, your team, your clients, and other stakeholders what your three main strengths are. You'll also have to ask for your opportunities areas; otherwise, the situation will get weird.

Once you get this information, try to find out the common aspects. Take them with some reserve, as they might not give you absolute certainty of your unique qualities, but it's the first approach.

2. The best place you can go for answers is yourself. Don't panic! Don't think you will have to spend the next ten years in an armchair analyzing your past and every action you've taken. No. It's as easy as thinking about what you enjoy most about your job.

Just watch yourself for a few days. Ready? Here are the four keys with which you will be able to know accurately and quickly what your precious talents are—those that make you absolutely unique and unrepeatable.

Key 1: Your Spontaneous Reactions

Try to note what your first reactions to the things you face are. Whether you find yourself in a stressful or everyday situation, you can learn a lot about your talents by noticing your initial reactions.

Put aside the thoughts that tell you that you should react in a certain way. The truth is that there is no correct way to respond to what happens to us. The universe doesn't wait for the perfect answer; it longs for *your* reply, the one you can only give.

Without considering if it's okay or not, record your first inner reaction. For instance, one hectic day, one of your collaborators calls you to tell you that his son is sick and can't show up. What is the first thing that goes through your mind? You ask if he needs any help for his child to recover soon—which would speak of great empathy—but perhaps not, and that is fine. You may think about how to delegate his stuff to guarantee the outcome, which would show you are results oriented. As you can see, there is no answer better than another, only *your* answer matters.

An excellent exercise to give you a better idea is to observe your friends when they meet in a restaurant for dinner. What does each one do? What motivates them?

- ✓ Perhaps one is asking if everyone is happy with the place and how they feel (empathic).
- ✓ Another is sharing a new anecdote (communicator).
- ✓ Another, who was late, offered to pay the bill to try to compensate (a sense of fairness).
- ✓ A fourth one tries to divert the conversation from hot topics among his friends (harmonious).
- ✓ There might be someone who is trying to sit next to someone whom he thinks can help him strengthen his work (ability to relate).
- ✓ Another calls the waiter and demands better service for all (command).

You make about 240,000 decisions a year, practically all of them based on your talents. They are therefore undoubtedly a comprehensive and valuable source of information.

Key 2: Your Yearnings

Your longings are like a detective's clues: they reveal the presence of talent, especially when they come from your childhood.

That voice within that tells you, "What I would truly like is to do a job that will impact positively on many people's lives" or "If I could have a beautiful flower shop" or "If I had a sports training center." As crazy as it may sound, that may be a significant clue to recognizing your talents. It may mean you genuinely want a flower shop or a gym, but it may also mean those places or activities involve something special that might enrich your professional career. Now you'll discover why.

Past or present, these longings tell us about your favorite synaptic connections, the most vital ways your brain works that have a magnetic influence on you. You simply cannot resist them; you feel their attraction, and therefore, you should think of these longings.

It is likely that since you were a child, you have been inclined to certain things. While your brother was playing with the dog in the yard, perhaps you were disassembling the hose to see how it worked.

Some find these clues from a very young age, such as Matt Damon and Ben Affleck, who, at ten, were looking for a quiet place in their school cafeteria to talk about their latest acting projects. Over time they wrote the screenplay for *Good Will Hunting*, which won them an Oscar.

At the age of thirteen, Pablo Picasso was already attending an art school for adults. Frank Gehry, one of the great architects of our time, made intricate models on the living room floor out of bits of wood from his father's business.

Of course, there are examples of children, like Wolfgang Amadeus Mozart, encouraged by their parents as soon as their talents were discovered. The potential for genius is within us as much as within them.

In some, social and financial pressures suffocate these desires. Others just need to go through different experiences to find ways to make themselves shine later in life. There are many great examples of late-career successes, like the following.

- ✓ Morgan Freeman got his first significant role when he was fifty-two.
- ✓ Ray Kroc was fifty-two when he bought McDonald's and grew it into the world's biggest fast-food franchise.
- ✓ Anna Mary Robertson Moses started painting at seventy-eight. One of her paintings sold for $1.2 million in 2006; previously, she was a housekeeper and farmer.
- ✓ Donald Fisher was forty when he opened the first Gap store in San Francisco. He had no experience in retail.

- ✓ Carlos Prieto, a successful engineer and economist from the Massachusetts Institute of Technology, later became a famous cellist.
- ✓ There are hundreds of examples, such as Taikichiro Mori, Jonah Peretti, Harland Sanders, and many others.

The important thing is that wherever you are, meeting your talents will be like getting on a bullet train that will take you as far as you want at full speed and will fill your job and life with joy.

You don't need to change career paths, although you may find you want to do so. You just need to use your talents wherever you decide to use them. If you see that they seem outlandish or even contrasting for an executive of a Fortune 500 company, don't be alarmed. You're a few pages away from discovering how to turn them into this bullet train we discussed.

Key 3: What You Learn Very Quickly

Longings don't always call all of us, so don't worry if this is your case. Sometimes talent calls us in another way.

Let's say you're in the middle of an important meeting. All your peers are talking about the complex implementation of a vital strategy to achieve the quarterly results. Suddenly, something ignites a spark within you, and you see everything with absolute clarity. Nothing is complicated anymore. You have the perfect picture. You know which projects are a priority, when they should be implemented, and what the critical success factors are. You even know who should participate in them. All you want is to run to get everything done.

The speed with which we understand and learn something reveals not only the presence of talent but its extraordinary power. It's the third key to finding your talents.

Think of the times when you have learned something new or managed to understand a very complex problem or situation in a short time. Recall those specific occasions when you have felt free and excited, like playing while learning. In fact, it may even be happening right now, so pay attention. Here are more clues.

A straightforward way to recognize when you are learning from your talent is that your movements and thoughts quickly lose that slowness typical of the beginner and acquire a speed and depth that you could not even imagine. You leave your colleagues behind, go ahead, reach conclusions long before the others and even object to the "expert" on the subject. Many times your solutions and proposals are more powerful and elegant. The attraction is so strong that you can't wait to put it into practice.

Whether you are good at selling an idea or a product, making presentations, developing designs and campaigns, developing a strategic plan, conducting interviews, organizing events, or establishing financial policies, if you have felt what I am talking about here, you will be able to identify the talent, or talents, that made it possible.

Key 4: Your Greatest Gratifications

Picture your brain. It's full of thousands of paths where all the information you might need, from tying your shoes to a complex strategy, travels at 268 miles per hour. All those are the connections between the billions of neurons—the synaptic connections. Just as you have your favorite ways to get to the movies, home, or to meet your friends, your brain also has preferences for certain roads or superhighways.

These pathways are the most robust synaptic connections designed to make us feel good when we use them. When you feel great doing an activity, there is a very high probability that you are using one of these superhighways, which is one of your signature talents.

Marcus Buckingham[11] interviewed thousands of top performers for his research on individual strengths. He found that a vast range of activities and outcomes makes people happy, but they all share the enjoyment of seeing a challenge in life and overcoming it (2001, 79). The most exciting thing is that this challenge means something different to each person. Buckingham has taken this concept further; he affirms that love is key to career success. He

---

[11] The co-author of *Now, Discover Your Strengths*, one of the first approaches to talent and an important guide.

says, "if you have no love for any of your work then you won't be creative, innovative, or resilient." (Buckingham 2022, 42).

The name of my company in some countries is "Love your job." If you truly want to feel fully alive and enthusiastic about your life and job, visit www.happinesspathways.com. I'll personally walk you through the journey to remove all your stress, fears, and anxiety to help you attain complete professional fulfillment, financial freedom, peace of mind, and life enjoyment.

Talents and Love Are in Details

Now you will see how diverse and specific talents are.

- ✓ Some enjoy achieving an infinitesimal improvement in their chosen sport that most of us would not recognize.
- ✓ Others enjoy bringing order out of chaos.
- ✓ For others, it is a pleasure to host a fancy event.
- ✓ Some love cleaning and smile while vacuuming. There is a maid at a Walt Disney hotel who has been cleaning the same rooms for twenty-one years and is happy doing it.

What could you learn from this? How could this cleaning lady's experience help you become a more successful CEO or a great regional IT head?

The truth is that although persistence is not a highly valued talent, it leads to outstanding achievements. Judge for yourself.

More than fourteen years after he became the number one tennis player in the world, Roger Federer returned to the top. He was ranked number one by the Association of Tennis Professionals for 310 weeks, including a record of 237 weeks, and finished as the year's top player five times. He retired as the greatest player of all time. He remained at the top seventy-seven weeks longer than Jimmy Connors' streak in the 1970s.

Do you like Snoopy? Me too! It may surprise you that Charles M. Schulz, a shy boy who drew comics for children, managed to make Snoopy one of the favorite characters of young and old. He drew the comic strip for forty-one years.

More Inspiration

Here are some other examples that might inspire you.

- ✓ Some are lovers of ideas.
- ✓ Some need to exceed their records.
- ✓ Others feel empty if they don't outperform their peers.
- ✓ For others, only learning has meaning.
- ✓ Others find purpose in life only if they help others.
- ✓ Some even enjoy rejection because it gives them a chance to demonstrate their persuasiveness.

Pay close attention to the things that give you gratification. They can be big things or very subtle details. It doesn't matter. Don't censor them or limit them because they are not what you must have. Explore them because they are there your talents. Honor them.

Online Assessment

Your executive talent compass

If you want to take a first glimpse at your talents, we have prepared an online evaluation that will undoubtedly make this task more accessible to you.

Visit it, and you will enter a new world of self-discovery in one minute. Enjoy!

Your Executive Talents

Online Assessment

Career Enlighten Academy

Access here
www.careerenlightenacademy.com/exectalents/

For those who know how to look, there are always signs.

—Kate Morton

Your exposure
Beyond personal branding

If there's something you need to know to have a successful career is that it's not about you, it's not about now, and it's not about what you've done.

It's all about the future: your future bosses and what you will create for them.

Most personal branding services focus on creating a polished executive image but lack the two most important facts. It's not about creating a rock star—a shell that's exactly a copy of anyone else; it's about:

Creating a solution for someone who is struggling with something that needs to be solved immediately.

Building a differentiation strategy centered on your uniqueness.

Can you imagine any of the top brands without a differentiation strategy? They would all look the same and use the same slogans, models, and logos. That's the exact mistake we make with our profiles, CVs, and interviews—in short, with our positioning strategies. The result? We camouflage with everyone else to the point that we become "correct" and invisible.

In this chapter, there are many elements you can use to create a genuinely unique positioning strategy that will guarantee all eyes on you.

Three Success Factors

Let's start with the three key points you need to watch closely.

1. You need a strong executive positioning strategy that works beyond your current professional status.

Most executives do not only forget to have a strategy to increase their positioning and visibility; sometimes, they carry out the actions that worked a few years ago, only to face the new market reality, which is more complex than ever.

Sometimes we also forget that the positioning strategy applies not only to a job search. It is just as important to apply it to your daily life within a company, especially if you want to grow and get exciting career opportunities.

2. That strategy involves any interaction with your current and future bosses.

It applies to each and every contact you have with them: your résumé, presentations, executive committee participation, emails, interviews, and any other vital interactions. All these elements need to send a consistent, clear, and convincing message that stands out.

3. Neither your positioning strategy nor its main elements is about you.

As said, it's always about the benefit your future bosses will obtain if they hire or promote you. Maybe this last key point is the most important one.

Of course, your strategy is nourished by your experience, background, qualifications, and achievements. However, it is a professional campaign whose objective is your future boss. If we only focus on the basics, it's like thinking that the pieces of an airplane are the elements that make the maneuvering and motion possible. In fact, it's the aerodynamic design and the pilot's talent that make the flight possible and that take us anywhere in the world in a matter of hours.

Similarly, your executive positioning campaign focuses on what talents and abilities you have to offer to your new or future boss.

The Most Expensive Mistake

It may seem easy to write and discuss the results we will create for our future bosses, but the truth is far more complex.

I have had the opportunity to advise hundreds of executives in being promoted, hired, and expatriated in high-executive positions at the most important global companies. Even the most senior ones find it very difficult to immerse themselves in their experiences and see beyond the deck to identify the depth and uniqueness of the results they can create.

We are used to seeing our professional backgrounds as a series of events and, in the best of cases, some isolated results that make much sense to us but often fail to convey our value to our future bosses.

Thus, being focused on ourselves, we fail to identify what the other person—the hiring manager—needs to see and hear to give us the positions we want. Our stories become stories told from us to us when they should be centered and focused on whoever is in front of us hearing it.

Your Audience Is Your Future Boss

The perspective you require may be almost the opposite of what you probably do today. Your hiring manager or future boss is looking for evidence of the results you can create. Don't focus on your responsibilities exclusively.

Look for what you achieved: how much you were able to produce and what distinguishes those achievements rather than how you carried them out. Focus on the deliverables, concrete objectives and key results (OKRs), and key performance indicators (KPIs) that you achieved, not on a list of typical competencies.

Even the most numerically-oriented executives have great difficulty performing this type of analysis since it goes beyond numbers; it's focused on the value the person has created and, therefore, the value he or she can make for a future boss.

In addition to this issue, trying to get to the hiring manager's perspective is not easy since he or she is in another part of the organization seeing things in a very different way. Therefore, looking for results can be hard to do from where we are. The difficulty is understandable, and coupled with the fact that no one has taught us how to do it.

Make a Correct Positioning Strategy

Making a positioning strategy is a unique experience. My coachees and students are amazed when they see the breadth, depth, and the enormous value their talents and expertise can create for their future positions and key stakeholders. It can turn everything in their favor when the other person is deciding who to hire or promote.

Creating a comprehensive strategy that underlies your talents and all the branding elements you need, from your résumé to your job-getting commercial,[12] and conveys all the value you can generate might be a gigantic task. Still, once it's achieved, the results are extraordinary. It becomes easier to communicate a genuine approach that speaks directly to all that you can do for your future bosses, without internal voices blocking the process, without becoming someone you're not, or feeling uncomfortably salesy.

All this is especially important when actively seeking a new challenge or trying to secure your current position and use it as a growth platform.

There are other critical strategic skills to master related to political savviness, cultural traits, allies, and stakeholder mapping, just to mention a few.

---

[12] As explained in Chapter 10.

Part IV

Powerful Positioning Strategies

There's no rejection; there's only feedback.

—Brian Tracy[13]

---

[13] While at a Top Coaching Congress in San Diego, California in 2010, I had the privilege to share the stage with him and other prominent figures.

Self-appraisal

How effective is your positioning and career strategy?

> When you can measure what you are speaking about,
> you know something about it; when you cannot
> express it in numbers, your knowledge is of a
> meagre and unsatisfactory kind.
>
> —William Thomson Kelvin

Do you remember this statement?[14] In career and executive coaching, I find many cases in which people don't improve as much as they could simply because they don't use the right tools or are not sufficiently aware.

That's why this self-appraisal is such a special gift for you. Nobody guides us or gives feedback on our positioning and career strategy, critical parts of living a whole life.

Perhaps one of the greatest blessings I have received in all these years has been the opportunity to touch hundreds of people's lives—I certainly hope yours, too! It has been a blessing to help them enrich their perspectives, transform

---

[14] Usually attributed to Peter Drucker, it's from Wiliam Thomson Kelvin, a brilliant British physicist and mathematician.

their realities (how they live in the present), and build extraordinary futures that, most of the time, only existed in their minds.

This three-minute self-appraisal will give you an initial understanding of where you are, what you can count on, and what you need to strengthen if you are going to reach your goals easier, faster, and without all the time, effort, and wear and tear it usually implies.

Your Positioning and Career Strategy

Self-Appraisal

Career Enlighten Academy

Access here
www.careerenlightenacademy.com/howeffectiveisyourstrategy/

Now that we have the first diagnosis, let's dive into the subject.[15]

---

[15] If you want a deeper diagnosis, we may soon open a few spots to work with me or one of my senior career strategists on a one-on-one free career speed-up session, if the schedule helps us. It will be a limited-time opportunity and just for a select group of professionals and executives who are genuinely committed to growing and achieving their goals. If this is your case, sign up here for the waitlist: www.careerenlightenacademy.com/waitlist

Your job-getting commercial
Leverage your expertise

If you're getting poor results, you have a poor strategy. It's not that you're not good enough; you only need to learn new tricks, that's all.[16]

Most people struggle with assertive communication. If this is your case, you'll find this tool extremely helpful.

Remember the elevator pitch? What if you could have a technique like that, not only for a specific project and business presentation, but summed up in a statement that includes all your experience, expertise, and potential in a way that talks directly to your potential hiring managers in your company or elsewhere?

Having a tailored-made phrase ready to apply in different situations in your professional career will get you a "wow" response and a "how do you do

---

[16] In this the book, you'll find plenty of resources to work with this inner voice that tells you you're not good enough (refer specifically to Chapter 19 in Part VI). If you're like most people, you may need help to eliminate it completely so you can thrive. If that's you, that's okay; you're not alone. Visit www.happinesspathways.com or send a direct email to talktoyardena@careerenlightenacademy.com, and I'll be happy to provide you the help you need. You may also want to send a WhatsApp to our helpline: +52 (55) 5436-3989 (English and Spanish).

that" kind of interest. It would be advantageous and valuable, right? It will undoubtedly position you with your bosses infallibly.

We lose many opportunities to sell our work and add value to our professional images. Commonly, the moments of truth take us by surprise, and we are not prepared to give our best answers. Our minds run on data, events, and situations. Ultimately, we answer in a hurry about what makes more sense and might seem relevant to the company. We fall short.

Why Does It Fail?

Our answers rarely share our value to its full extent, and often fail to awaken the curiosity and interest of our audience to know more about us and our potential.

Even the highest executives need to polish and develop this skill. Beyond that, the fact is that the decision to include certain executives in an aggressive development and succession plan does not only come from the results we create. What to do?

Create a Positive and Lasting Impression

One way I like to work on this topic with my coachees is this. Imagine I invite you to a thirty-second interview on the radio. What would you say to having five headhunters calling you with appealing opportunities when you finish your speech? Sounds impossible? It is easier than you imagine.

Play with me for a minute, and it will dazzle you.

Four Strategic Questions

Think about your job and how what you do highlights your unique talents.[17] Review these questions, and find the ultimate answer from the most strategic point of view.

1 What is the main objective of your job?	It may seem obvious, but it slips our minds on more than one occasion! Think about a. The ultimate reason for your position to exist in the company, e.g., why they hired you, whether in your current or last job; and b. What they expect from you, even though they didn't tell you. It is not always what's written in your job description or what you have in mind. If you are looking for a new job, this is the reason that will trigger your hiring.
2 What benefits will the company obtain when you achieve this goal?	It is the value your job creates for the operational and business results. It may help to ask yourself, *Why is it important that I achieve this significant objective? What implications would it have for the company if I did not?*
3 Specifically, what actions have you taken to achieve it?	You have taken these actions to achieve that goal and guarantee the company gets the expected results.
4 What are your results?	Show concrete and numeric results. These will communicate that you achieved, exceeded, or are on the way to attaining that objective. Use actual data and reference numbers. Any initial parameter or benchmark will highlight your achievements: relevant market surveys, local, regional or global rankings, and so on.

---

[17] Review the chapter "Your signature talents" in the previous part.

Put It Together

Put together your answers and the information you gathered. Create a statement that doesn't exceed thirty seconds and that sounds like this.

I work to ensure the company attracts, develops, and retains the best talent in the market to guarantee the continuity of state-of-the-art organizational operations and actively contribute to exceeding business objectives.

I have implemented XYZ programs, and we have delivered ABC results.

Where
XYZ can be specialized and managerial training programs, talent growth best practices, total rewards strategies, talent management strategies, flex and hybrid working schemes, centers of excellence, and so on.

And
ABC may be low rotation, a high number of qualified candidates for critical positions, satisfaction and engagement improvement, a positive working environment, highly effective executive teams, and so on.

This example is for an HR head. You can use it as a template to create your own, adapting it to your area of expertise and making it even more specific by adding your data and details.

Pre-Written Job-Getting Commercials

We've also prepared some templates for other areas. You can get immediate access here: www.careerenlightenacademy.com/jobgettingcommercial

What Is Its Impact?

The job-getting commercial will always attract attention and will earn you the respect and interest of others because:

1. Identifying objectives and specific results position you as an assertive, results-oriented executive. Many people talk about "taking things beyond" or "closing the gap," but it's too vague.
2. You're talking to your bosses about their most significant interests and worries: the company's results and, therefore, their bonuses! But, shhh, don't tell anyone!
3. You explained concisely the actions you took to reach the objective. Realize you didn't talk about the multiple obstacles you found on the way. Most of the time, your bosses and inner clients, local, national, regional, or global, are not interested in how you did it, but they are interested in the result.
4. You've discussed the results in concrete and numeric terms, proving your absolute control of your team's performance and mastering the crucial numbers and KPIs of your area, the company, and the market.

These are other reasons why they will be eager to take you to a higher position. You represent lots of money for them!

What's Next?

Here is what you want to do.

Pick one of the job-getting commercials we've created for you and enrich it. Even better, create your own and practice it five or six times until you memorize it.

Then, think about places or situations in which you could use it in the next few days and see how people react and respond.

Observe how people start showing interest in your skills and work, asking for your contact information, and telling you about companies that could use someone just like you.

Use it in staffing, hunting, and job posting processes—or inside your company with your current bosses and evaluate the results!

Your résumé and social media
Entice your future bosses

*Why am I not getting the answer I want, even when I've worked
so hard on my résumé and LinkedIn profile?*

This question came up while I was conducting a masterclass on how to create an unbeatable résumé that gets you hired or promoted. Over 240 people from fifteen countries were trying to create a compelling CV and become visible and relevant in an overloaded, cybernetic world.

In twenty-seven years, I have had the opportunity to see hundreds of thousands of resumes from all areas, industries, countries, and executive levels you can imagine.

I have done it from three complementary perspectives.

1. I led talent attraction teams during my work as HR head within Fortune 500 companies.
2. As a headhunter for major global corporations, I squeezed the market to find the best talent.
3. In my coaching practice, I advised executives on how to face all the challenges that HR specialists, headhunters, and hiring managers will place in the way.

The objective was to help them achieve their perfect jobs and fits quickly, whether their goals were to grow up the leadership ladder or something else.

During all this time, I have found this is the most common concern most executives have: how to create a powerful CV that will engage their future hiring managers, headhunters, and HR specialists.

It's hard for even those executives who are supposed to have know-how. Most of my marketing and HR coachees are surprised by how difficult it is for them, too; they find that even when they have or know some tools, it's pretty challenging to apply them for their benefit.

If you feel it's not your thing, you're not the only one. I've been there. Before I learned the tools and strategies I'll share with you, I felt utterly lost. Your CV is another essential you want to work with a real expert on.

The first step to moving toward a résumé that will increase your positioning and visibility is understanding how to avoid the main pitfalls.

Three Pitfalls That Block Your Progress

What we'll see now will reset the way you look at your résumé. You are going to set new expectations for yourself, and these will help you create a new mindset as well.

1. Thinking that you'll have it figured out overnight

I say this repeatedly to my coachees: everything we're teaching you is a process, an overhaul of the old ways of doing things and expecting things to happen.

Until you dive deep enough into the critical aspects of your talents, skills, and experience, you cannot get to a place where you have complete clarity on your unique value proposition. It's not easy to discover the talents and traits that make you unique as a top executive in your area. They also are the backbone of a compelling positioning and personal branding strategy rooted in talent and results (not only for your résumé but your interviews and the whole process).

When we're able to transmit effectively what only we can contribute to a team and a company, we start building momentum and start having lagging indicators: get people's responses, hook people, and awaken their interest to have honest conversations with you, to call you to schedule an interview, or to answer your messages.

2. Focusing your résumé on ATS (Applicant Tracking Systems)

One of the global trends today in attracting new talents for leading companies is the applications and software that promise to streamline the recruiting and hiring process from applicant tracking and engagement to interviewing and onboarding. Up to 98 percent of Fortune companies use ATS.

To be found by one of these robots implies an accurate emphasis on keywords, skills, job titles, educational background, and so on. It also requires having a specific template that is scan friendly.

This tendency has only doubled the degree of complexity for candidates. While you need to ensure that you're visible to the robot, the key to success is guaranteeing that you're relevant to a human being.

Your hiring manager is a person who is seeking to meet a specific need. You can't ignore it; you need to address it. You need to learn how to connect with that need. First, understand that even though they are top corporate executives, they have their concerns and dreams, and they are looking for something—not only to fill in a position but to get specific great results.

To build a bridge that connects with them, you will have to do a more profound exercise than just having the keywords for a machine. You need to know precisely what this person wants to see on your résumé to see you as the complete response and solution to their needs and concerns. What is going to make them turn to your LinkedIn profile and think you can be a good bet. Having this in mind is essential.

3. Caring for what people think

This is a major issue and applies to many topics regarding your positioning. It's something that we all face all the time, and we have this mental block of:

> "What is my family going to say?"
> "What will my colleagues think if I update my résumé and LinkedIn profile with a more 'aggressive' positioning strategy?"

To avoid these situations, we usually do the same thing we see other people doing; the sad truth is that we get the same poor results.

The real question is why do you worry about them? Are they going to hire, promote, or give you the job, the salary, and the fulfillment you want?

You will have to decide between two things you may not like and choose the one you dislike the least.

One is that there may be people who feel annoyed if you gain visibility, in the sense of:

> "Why does this person want to be successful and stand out?"
> "How dare this person want a better position and to make more money?"

One of the options is to take care of those kinds of responses, do nothing, and stay where you are so you don't disturb or conflict with anyone.

Most of the time, we have seen that people who are going to be offended are not the people who will promote you to a higher job or hire you for the position you want. At some point, you must choose between how much it's worth to keep happy people who are not paying your bills or giving you any career opportunities and how much your growth and happiness is worth.

They are people who, in general, feel you are competing with them and don't want to be left behind, so you must overcome that. It's difficult because feeling concerned about standing out is normal and natural.[18]

We all have these kinds of blocks, and if you can't stop them, you become a prisoner of your concern for how others see you and what they are going to think

> "What if they think it's ridiculous? Or too much?"

Then you don't take action and prefer to stay in a safe place where your CV and LinkedIn profile blend in, and you become invisible.

And that's precisely the result.

When we can master our emotional intelligence and psychology, we can speed up all our career goals. That's why working with an expert who helps eliminate all these blockages is so important.

> Once you start living according to other people's rules,
> going along with what other people think, your
> soul shrivels and dies.
>
> —Katherine Pancol

---

[18] You'll find interesting insight from recent studies regarding this issue in the chapter "It's not only about money" from Part II.

The biggest three pitfalls in CVs

A few days ago, my team and I launched a free campaign to explore with executives what precisely their CVs convey and how we can help them improve their CVs.

It was a great success. We received hundreds of requests from executives of all levels, from C-suite, country presidents, general directors, directors, senior managers, and managers—in short, from different backgrounds, but all with the desire to receive expert feedback on their résumés.

Some shared with us their need to improve their CVs as they want to move to another company. They felt overwhelmed, undervalued, and without growth opportunities, but they were doubtful that their CVs were attractive enough to explore new opportunities in the job market.

Others were actively seeking jobs and felt discouraged because their CVs were not attracting any attention. Others commented that they participated in long processes that did not prosper, much less provided feedback.

Most of them had done what we commonly do: look for CV forms online or through colleagues and friends, copy what we see others do on social networks, or use what we have seen and think is "correct" in the CVs of other people. In short, most worked without expert help. Ultimately, they realized that their CVs did not reflect their true potential, experience, and value.

Avoid Costly Mistakes

The truth is that no one teaches us how to write a compelling résumé, and most of the time, we have never received any feedback from a true expert. I think feedback will significantly help you, especially if you are committed to your professional growth and know the importance of having a high-impact CV.

1. It does not immediately convey your full potential and value

Your CV will be scanned and evaluated in five to six seconds maximum. From there, they will define whether or not you continue in the selection process.

Has it happened to you that you get stuck in this first filter? They asked for your résumé, and you never had more news?

2. Lack of compelling and relevant achievements and KPIs

Describing achievements is not enough. What counts is doing it assertively and precisely.

John E. Smith Jr., an influential business professional, says that a resume is a personal sales organizer; its function is to inform and sell what only its author knows perfectly. Most candidates don't know this, which is why almost all report but don't sell. Good candidates make this mistake very often. (1997, 86).

3. Lack of clear strategy and positioning

We miss out on higher-level opportunities because of poor positioning that doesn't drive our growth. Part of the secret is knowing how to balance algorithms with getting people's attention by highlighting what is crucial.

The most successful companies—Apple, Tesla, Coca-Cola, for example—have unique positioning. In all cases, we are very clear about what we will get from them and that they are the best choice.

Your interviews
Win the job without sweating

When you are invisible, one of the main effects is that you apply for positions that seem perfect, and although you would swear that the interviews went very well, they selected someone else. Worse, has it happened to you not just on one isolated occasion but at various times?

When I was anxious to leave a company that seemed attractive but had a toxic environment that sucked me in and drained me, I was so desperate that I went to literally hundreds of interviews.

How could an expert in attracting and selecting talent not be able to get a job at another company? It was embarrassing. It was a tough immersive training field that left me with bulletproof strategies and techniques learned and designed from the other side of the desk. Not many of my fellow coaches share that same frustration and expertise.

I learned every must, every shortcut, and every cost you can't afford, but above all, I realized I was doing it all wrong.

Career Enlighten

When You Do the Right Things the Wrong Way

Even though most executives know that obtaining jobs depends to a greater extent on their abilities to have successful interviews, they don't know what to do to advance in the processes and have the desired proposals in their pockets.

Sometimes, something prevents us from advancing beyond a certain point; an invisible force is determined to sabotage our progress. Yet this phenomenon has been studied and documented[19]; we still get few strategies to effectively take steps to eliminate this evil force and leap.

What Distinguishes a Successful Interview from a Failed One?

The point is that we do not know what distinguishes a successful interview from a failed one. We are even less ready to face a selection process successfully. This is the actual glass ceiling. As long as we don't manage to equip ourselves with the best strategies, the job we want will be unattainable, a good wish. Every month without achieving it, we lose lots of money and valuable time for our career growth and improvement.

We rarely realize that the biggest problem is that we do not know our achievements and talents deeply enough. Consequently, we cannot get the best out of them to position ourselves and strengthen our candidacies.

Some people do excellent jobs of gathering key company information; however, today, that is insufficient. It worked some years ago when the market was different, and having specific data was an added value.

Today, anyone can get hundreds of data points online in seconds, so it is no longer a differential. Moreover, no matter how much information you can gather, your interviewer will always have more. He or she owns that information, you see? By that, I do not mean that you stop doing it. You need

---

[19] Gay Hendricks in *The Big Leap* (2009), Tal Ben-Shahar in *Happier* (2007), and Mihaly Csikszentmihalyi in *Good Business: Leadership, Flow, and the Making of Meaning* (2004) all speak about the now well-known "glass ceiling," or the "upper limit barrier."

to be in the game; however, that won't get you picked for the position. It's just another basic you need to cover.

In a recent interview, three successful female CEOs who reached the top of Facebook, Danone, and Dupont, talked about what has worked for them[20].

For them, what made the difference was

- ✓ trusting in themselves;
- ✓ taking risks; and
- ✓ especially not waiting until someone discovered their talents.

The first and last points are crucial, and things I constantly work on with my clients. We work on trust in ourselves as part of strengthening and mastering emotional intelligence. It is also a collateral result of the work of discovering and polishing one's talents and achievements.

When executives come to me for help with this topic, they are surprised and amazed by the quick results they get. Do not worry if you still do not know how to achieve the job you want; you are not alone, and you're not the only one who has been there. You would be surprised to hear the comments of many of my highest-level clients.

> "I would never have gotten the job without these strategies."
> "I managed to see my experience from a new perspective to transmit all my value with clarity and forcefulness."
> "No one had taught me any of this."

For now, let's focus on what makes the difference.

Build a Strong Case

As candidates, we leave too much to the imagination of our interviewers. We do not realize that we are the only ones in a position to understand our trajectory and make our achievements shine fully.

---

[20] El Financiero Site 2019.

Be careful. We think we are only competing for positions when we go to job interviews at other companies. The reality is that within our companies, we are under evaluation most of the time. All the time, we are applying for other positions and many times even for our jobs. Daily, we compete in a invisible talent contests that will actually occur once or twice a year before the organization and talent review committee. As soon as the company considers we no longer meet the profiles or expected results, our careers will suffer unflattering consequences.

If You Really Want to Stand Out

You need to become an expert in your trajectory, learn to make it shine, and shield it against any doubt, error, or questioning.

No trajectory is perfect, so relax! The important thing is that there is a way to transform any experience into a brilliant career that excites headhunters, recruiters, and decision-makers who can give you everything you want.

The Unbeatable Formula

Experts and researchers have found various crucial aspects[21]. When I analyzed them, I observed similar patterns. After that, I created what I call my unbeatable formula.

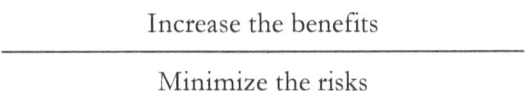

$$\frac{\text{Increase the benefits}}{\text{Minimize the risks}}$$

The probability of being promoted or hired increases exponentially when the benefit of hiring or promoting you is substantially more significant than the risk of doing it. When the movement is about to happen within your company, you need to consider the risk of leaving your current assignment.

---

[21] Donald Asher in *Who Gets Promoted, Who Doesn't, and Why* (2007), and Joe Dispenza in *Breaking The Habit of Being Yourself: How to Lose Your Mind and Create a New One* (2013).

Without a doubt, it is difficult to find the actual benefit and differential advantages of our histories and talents and how to minimize the risks that specialists and recruiters can see from miles away. Anyone who has created his or her CV knows it can be like trying to get to a good destination on a winding road in thick fog.

The real difficulty, and the critical factor for this formula to work, is our ability to convey it coherently and consistently during the whole process and every stage of the selection process or daily observation and evaluations within our companies.

Part V

Make more money

What for one person may be a prudential distance for another is an abyss.

—Haruki Murakami

Day in and day out, we watch the news about multimillionaires and how they spend and gain incredible amounts of money like they were pennies. We saw Elon Musk lose 30 billion dollars on a Tweet or 100 billion dollars walking away from a business deal. He even holds the record for losing more money in a day, yet, according to *Forbes*, he earned 150 billion dollars in a year, from 2021 to 2022. He has also become the most powerful man in the world to this moment.

Most of us will never see these numbers, not even in several lives. Yet, he seems so relaxed—and even amused—with those gains and losses.

Who's to say how much is a lot of money, and how much is a little money? As Einstein said about time, it's relative. We could apply this statement to cash—or not.

I want you to start thinking about what an ideal financial situation would be for you. What salary would you like to earn? What benefits, perks, and conditions would make you feel calm and well rewarded for everything you value?

I want you to multiply that amount by ten and notice what happens inside you, how you feel about it. There may be a part that feels excited and happy, but there may also be a part inside you that might feel uncomfortable with, even afraid of, this figure.

Don't worry if that happens. It's normal. We live in an ambivalent society. It makes us idealize people with money. Simultaneously, it fills our hearts and minds with doubts and feelings of guilt, unworthiness, and false loyalties that take us down. We think those wealth levels are only for a few selected people, but not us.

That is why, when it comes to money, we have thousands of emotions and beliefs that, most of the time, block our way to wealth and our relationship with money.[22]

Once you clean up all of them, you'll be able to reach the financial freedom you want, whatever that means to you.

What your beliefs are, how to clean them up, and where that might take you is something we'll work on in this book. For now, I invite you to sit calmly and keep on reading. What you'll find out here might forever change your relationship with money, wealth, and abundance.

You may also discover that you don't have to choose and leave what's essential for you—that the following statement is not necessarily true, at least not for you.

> People always say: "I never see you at the club."
> I reply, "I never see you at the bank."
>
> —Grant Cardone

---

[22] According to specialized surveys, 59 percent of American workers said they are apprehensive about negotiating salary. Most interesting is the fact that the overwhelming top response was a primary emotion we've all faced: fear of rejection. 43 percent of respondents said they're scared of being rejected and feeling like they're not good enough. 15 percent feared they'd be fired (Salary Site 2013).

Are you underpaid?

After twenty-seven years as an HR head, headhunter, and senior executive coach for the most important global companies, I've seen many executives jeopardize their growth and jobs due to poor career and salary negotiation processes.

The Nightmare

One of the worst things that can happen is discovering that we are underpaid. We see that another person holding the same level in the company or the same position in the market earns much more. Maybe we realize we don't make the right salary that fully reflects all our experience, expertise, and potential. Other times, we see people who enjoy a more attractive and relaxed lifestyle. Even with higher qualifications or broader experience, we don't get to the level we want.

It might be shocking, right? Sadly, it's a more common situation than we would like. The first question that arises in our heads is, *What can I do about it?*

Salary negotiation is one of the most challenging parts of the corporate world and is almost taboo in most cultures and countries. It's an emotionally challenging moment for every executive, and that's why most people won't get into asking for more money.[23]

The Risks

Salary negotiation is so difficult to deal with correctly and requires sophisticated skills and strategies (if we want the best outcome). Few people master them, and even fewer are willing to teach us or share their valuable techniques with us. If we don't do it correctly, we take unnecessarily high-cost risks.

Some days ago, one of my corporate clients, an HR lead from a top pharma company that last year grew from the third position to the first position in their market, decided to withdraw the job offer they made to a candidate for the regional IT lead position. He requested an additional 23 percent raise to join the company, and his approach was so poor that they decided he wasn't the right person for such a strategic role.[24]

The Decision

It's easy to think, "if those are the risks, is it a good idea—or even possible—to negotiate an increase in your offer or a raise in your salary, especially right now?"

What to do if you want a higher salary and an attractive executive compensation package? Will you sit back until the company finally sees your total value and come up with a new proposal or raise letter?

---

[23] This is true even though the numbers are promising and point out that the risk is minimal if we know how to handle the negotiation in favorable terms. We'll learn more in the footnotes ahead.

[24] In his case, the company had already offered him a 30 percent salary increase plus an additional 50 percent annual bonus. According to Salary.com, 73 percent of employers agree they are not offended when people negotiate. Furthermore, "a whopping 84% said they always expect job applicants to negotiate salary during the interview" (Salary Site, 2013). We must take advantage, learn how to work with our emotions, and get the best negotiation strategies to ensure the desired results. If you want to learn more proven and ready-to-use techniques, you can find more information here: bit.ly/CareerAndSalaryGrowth.

Of course not.

Before starting a negotiation, preparing yourself is vital. Having a robust strategy guarantees you the best result and doesn't jeopardize the new opportunity or your current role and image.

The Three Main Pitfalls

These are three of the critical factors that will prevent you from making costly mistakes when it comes to salary negotiations.

1. Timing

Even the most confident, competent high-level executive cringes at the thought of navigating salary and compensation negotiations, and most don't know precisely when to broach the subject.

While it's natural to feel concerned about your current or potential employer's salary range or benefits offers to a specific executive level, you'll need to do several things to strengthen your image and application before discussing any offer-related issues. The worst thing you can do is jump into it early.

2. Wording

This is probably one of the most essential and valuable tools you will take advantage of throughout your executive career.

To master it, you must use the precise formula I've developed after helping thousands of executives negotiate hiring terms and raises over decades[25]. One of the prominent parts of this formula is the wording. Only the words? Are you for real? No.

---

[25] During my career, in my different roles—as HR lead, coach, and headhunter—I've participated in and advised for successful salary negotiations for over 107 million dollars, including base salary, flex benefits, perquisites, working and work-life balance conditions, and expatriate terms.

These are the five critical elements you want to watch out for.

Element	Way to use it
Right words	Address specific topics. You want to use precise words to enrich your image and positioning before jumping to ask for the increase.
Correct order	Follow the precise order. You can't miss a step. Every step was designed to a) make your hiring or promoting manager eager to retain you; and b) give you an excellent and elegant way out in case there's no way to increase your offer, whether you decide to take it or leave it.
Right tone	The tone is one of the most challenging aspects of communication you may learn, but probably one of the most important.
Right pace and rhythm	When we get nervous, one of the ways our bodies and brains react is by trying to avoid or leave the risk situation as quickly as possible. We begin talking too fast, mumbling, and justifying ourselves and our motives. All these will make our listeners doubt if they made the right decision about us. There is a thin, risky line we need to watch closely all the time during interviews and, especially, during negotiations.
Right pauses	A critical and surprising element, it's the one that will take you to the longed higher financial freedom and peace.

When you master these five elements, you can

- ✓ Create the confidence you need;
- ✓ Build a safety net to eliminate any risk; and
- ✓ Strengthen your executive image to get the results you want.

3. Skills and Mindset

You have no idea how often I get my HR or commercial heads clients to say, "It's incredible how I can handle the most challenging negotiations for the company, but I can't do it regarding my career and salary."

As candidates or executives, we usually arrive at the negotiation as if it were business as usual and just another negotiation. What a colossal miscalculation.

Not every negotiation will require everyday skills or follow the same rules. A successful negotiation is about the value your current bosses and future employers perceive in you, and above all, it's about your mindset.

Never underestimate the power of having a powerful strategy and a strong mindset, and developing the skills you may need when discussing your salary and career. It will be your best bet in the long run.

The hidden truth

The hidden truth is that the number one mistake we often make regarding our salaries, bonuses, and benefits has nothing to do with them. It starts long before we sit down to discuss or negotiate with the company and is perhaps the cornerstone of our executive growth: our positioning[26].

When it comes to negotiating not only your salary but the terms that will give you the balance and life experience you want, working with a true expert will speed up and strengthen your positioning. Mastering the skills and strategies you need will be one of the most important investments you can make in your career.[27]

> With horizons, you have to do more than just look at them from afar; you have to walk towards them and conquer them.
>
> —Julio Cortázar

---

[26] Please refer to Chapter 8 in Part III, "Your exposure: beyond personal branding."
[27] You can see many success stories and some of the results we've created for many people and executives in my LinkedIn profile: www.linkedin.com/in/yardenak.

Are you suffering from invisible executive syndrome?[28]

I was watching a movie with my daughter, who is a huge comics fan, when she exclaimed, "Wouldn't it be amazing to have any of those powers?"

Of course! How amazing it would be if we could choose one and use it professionally. What would you do differently or change if you could move at super speed, or better yet, time travel? I can think of many things.

However, there is a superpower that, in fact, we sometimes use in real life even without realizing it.

Being Invisible

In real life, being invisible can become an absolute nightmare. We see it often: bunches of executives and professionals walking through their professional lives as if they were invisible.

---

[28] Thank you, Christian Mickelsen, for sharing this concept with me and for so much wisdom, ideas, and guidance.

What we need is just the opposite: not to go unnoticed. We need to have the best possible visibility and positioning, especially when we have executive careers to boost.

You want headhunters and hiring managers to quickly think of you (and of you above anyone else) when they need to fill a position that may interest you and will continue building your career. You also want to be recommended as a great candidate when other talent specialists and potential bosses are looking for someone strong for a top position.

The High Risk of Being Unnoticed

According to *Statista*, in 2021, LinkedIn had approximately 774.61 million global users[29], of which over 74.59% were in the twenty strongest economies worldwide.[30]

That's why it's so easy to be unnoticed and get lost in all this noise in the vast digital static.

Suddenly, you can even feel that you are wearing a kind of invisible cloak: it seems that the world is so busy with its own thing that nobody sees you, nobody responds to your efforts to connect, you lose essential processes, and interviews do not materialize; in short, there is simply no answer. Yet, it is worth the effort.

Just the Void, the Silence

Maybe we have great potential and excellent track records at the world's biggest companies. However, we still do not have the positions, levels, and financial stability to achieve the lifestyles we truly want.

---

[29] Degenhard, J. 2021. According to his forecast, the number of LinkedIn users in the World is projected to reach 1,034.56 million by 2025.
[30] Dixon, S. 2022.

Bringing an invisibility cloak has costly consequences at all levels.

- In our career growth, we do not find ways to open our ways to new positions—or at least, to the places that are most attractive to us. We lose opportunities that would have been key to our advancement.
- In our current positions, sometimes we do not achieve the results that the company expects from us. If we do, we do it with enormous sweat and tears because of the lack of positioning and internal allies. We feel isolated and demoralized, which increases the risk of falling into the dread freezer.

I've been there myself and know how exhausting and demoralizing it can be.[31] I remember when I tried to grow and reach a position that lived up to my potential and experience and how hard it was not to achieve it.

Beyond the frustration of the situation, it made me feel like a failure, especially when I saw other people—less prepared, more often than not—reach those levels with an ease that seemed surprising to me. It was shocking, and I'm not lying; I sometimes felt annihilated.

If you have experienced a similar situation that affects your professional and economic growth, believe me, you are not alone.

Many executives with tremendous value to offer don't know how to get their messages across to key people.

---

[31] If you didn't have the chance to read the introductory part of this book, I strongly recommend you read it now. I recount all the struggles I had to go through before I started growing and holding regional roles and global assignments. Mostly, I discuss how I came to know my true calling. I started making it my way of living and an incredibly successful business that has allowed me to exceed every wildest dream I've ever had. Do you know what that is like? I believe everyone has the right to pursue this kind of achievement. Maybe we don't know how to attain it, but that's precisely why we are here.

How to Break Free

That's one of the most important questions you could ask yourself. It doesn't have a simple or one-sided answer. I love talking and writing about our uniquenesses and talents, as I firmly believe that if we want to achieve greatness, we certainly can. However, we need to rely on those signature talents and our genius zones.

Part VI

Become unstoppable

Nothing should be taken for granted,
even if everybody believes it.

—Yuval Noah Harari

The treasure map is in your mind

One of the keys I would like to share with you today so you can transform into a highly requested executive is to put your vision on images.

Visualizing Is the Secret Weapon of the United States Army

Sounds absurd, right? The United States Army has incorporated these techniques as part of the training for their elite soldiers. If this can prepare soldiers for war, imagine what it can do for you.

Want to give it a try?

Think big: your ideal job, your family, that house you've always wanted, new trips, new challenges, new countries, and assignments. Think about the little moments: a concert, Sunday breakfast, walking your dog. Imagine yourself there.

How would you feel?
What would you think?
Who would you be?

Now imagine you have traveled ten years into the future. How would your life be? What would your thoughts be? Your days? Your feelings? Your ideas? Observe yourself and feel like that powerful person you wish to be.

As that person, what advice would you give yourself to make the journey easier?

Take your advice. Follow it. Start creating your treasure map and walking those routes leading you to the chest. Start running.

The secret relies on taking little actions in your daily life. Then, you could move mountains.

One last thing: be patient and diligent. Creating the professional life of your dreams takes time and energy, but it's worth it. Besides, your vision may be much closer than you imagine.

Who owns your career?

One of my clients recently shared his concern about his next career move with me, and he worried that the company might have a change plan that wasn't exactly what he wanted. This issue is one of the most common concerns I hear when I advise senior executives to optimize their next career steps.

A Double-Edged Knife

1. Inside your company

When we are inside the company, we worry

- that they will move us to positions we don't want;
- that colleagues will get the jobs we want, or worse, they bring in someone from another company;
- about how we are seen and our status; and
- perhaps the greatest of all concerns, that one day they will decide to do without us for whatever reasons: unforeseen changes, unattainable goals, or any other missteps.

2. Outside the company

When we are outside, first, the stories are not very different. Then, as time passes by, concerns accumulate, and family, social, economic, and professional pressures fall with more force. Then it becomes very intense. It is no longer just about achieving status or a position but about avoiding being ignored by the market at all costs, and the gap widens every day.

Playing the Right Move

The thing is, even with all these concerns, more often than not, we usually play a passive role when it comes to our careers. We think there's nothing we can do but wait to see what the company plans, and hopefully, it will match what we want. Other times, we believe we only have to limit ourselves to responding reactively to the few vacancies we find in a constantly changing market.

Nothing could be more wrong! We have much more power than we think.

The reality is that companies require talent, as it always has been. Moreover, it is likely that today more than ever, the market challenges tend to overwhelm companies. What has changed is that today they require different talent and are endowed with other tools. This does not mean they need younger or more mature talent; they require proven executives to achieve business objectives.

Companies expect trained executives ready to face whatever comes successfully.

I would love to say the opposite, but the truth is that companies will not see for us or our interests. It's hard but true. The company is programmed to seek its own goals and profit—nothing more.

To think otherwise is to be naive, especially in today's world, which is experiencing a fourth industrial revolution. According to *Deloitte*, Industry 4.0 "appears to be changing the way businesses function. It's ushering in a digital reality that may alter the rules of production, operations, workforce—even society." (Cotteleer and Sniderman 2017).

Remain Competitive in the New Market

Whenever an executive comes to me because he can't achieve what he wants, I ask some simple yet powerful questions that most of the time, he has never asked himself. We usually discover that he handed over the reins of his career to companies and that he had limited himself to doing what other people said or recommended. No one had taught him how to take charge and lead his career.

It happens at all levels. Even the best business schools teach us how to lead to achieve the company's desired results, but they do not give us the tools to achieve our own goals.

The most common mistake is to think that our results will speak for us and get us where we want. In reality, our results are the natural output that the company expects, and as soon as we achieve them, the company and bosses forget about them to face new goals and challenges. Our responsibility is to ensure that our results are valued and serve as platforms to achieve our professional goals. How do we do this?

Empower Yourself

The first step is to realize that no one will look after our personal goals, read our minds, or fulfill promises. When we eliminate these false expectations, we start to move forward.

You want to let go of the "pick me" passive and over-demanding attitude. It's not true that "they choose you," "they promote you," "they recognize you," and "they value you." If you hold any job within any aggressive competitive company, you do so because you generate big bucks. Give yourself more credit. Empower yourself. Be aware that you also choose, ask, recognize, value, and create your path.

When you take your power back, you can transmit your actual value to promote who you are and the results you create. Then companies will see you with other eyes, and you'll take your career into your hands and achieve any goal you want.

That is not as difficult as it seems. Several strategies and tools are specifically designed to facilitate achieving our career goals, and it's just a matter of knowing them and applying them correctly.

Get rid of the brain programming
That blocks you

Jorge is one of my favorite coachees. He leads a team of geniuses—literally! They are in charge of discovering extremely complex and high-speed market trends for one of the largest consumer packaged good companies in the world.

He was recently promoted to Global Head of Machine Learning Operations (MLOps) and Platforms. He has also gained incredible external recognition: *Forbes*, McKenzie, Gardner, and Snowflake are crazy about his growth and results. They have published articles, interviews, and business cases and granted him awards for his achievements.

These results don't come by chance; you must take the most brilliant actions to get there. Believe me; all great minds have developed their full potential with the help of great advisors.[32]

What you've achieved in your career is more than the sum of your results and the opportunities you've taken, or not taken, as we usually think. To a greater extent, it is also the result of how prepared your brain is to help you, or block you, in thriving and achieving significant success.

---

[32] I love this Ted Talk with Bill Gates and interview with Eric Schmidt: bit.ly/EricSchmidtBillGates

The neuroscientist Michael Merzenich has discovered that rewiring your brain could result in dramatic changes leading to success, as featured in the World Economic Forum Site (2016). Your mind can be your best buddy or your worst enemy. And if it's not wired correctly, it will hold you back from success in the worst moment when you have to seize the opportunity.

Recently I offered a masterclass entitled "Up The Leadership Ladder" at Smart Interviews.[33] People were shocked at how many high-cost mistakes they've unconsciously made that went far beyond not being hired or promoted. Still, they lost key opportunities that could have led them to something greater or set them on different paths.

The bottom line on mastering interviews and all the strategies you'll need to accelerate your growth is that you'll also have to get your brain ready to do the job to outpace your competition. Otherwise, your untamed mind will take control and leave you exactly where you are.

Even if you have the best personal branding strategy or excellent interview skills, it's not enough. Don't get me wrong; these are critical elements that we help our clients build, so they can have a powerful toolkit to strengthen their positioning and guarantee their progress. But they are only part of the holistic approach you'll need to get your career and life exactly where you want them to be. This is one of the main reasons our clients get fast and outstanding results.

Understanding how your brain is wired and how it was programmed is the first step in taking back control of your mind and career.

Reprogram Your Brain for Success

Even though you didn't control what was loaded in your brain at a particular moment[34], science shows us that you can take some actions to rewire your brain into a healthier one that will allow you to thrive in your job and career.

---

[33] You may follow me on LinkedIn (linkedin.com/in/yardenak/) and subscribe to our LinkedIn newsletter to participate in these events: bit.ly/UpTheLeadershipLadder.

[34] If you want to go deeper and get more detailed information and valuable tips, sign up at: www.careerenlightenacademy.com/brainseries.

You also want to avoid inevitable brain frustrations when turning the table on bad luck or adversity.

As negative information and feedback have an impact on your brain, the opposite is also true. When you're successful, that success gets into your head and changes it, according to Earl Miller from Massachusetts Institute of Technology, as shared in *Harvard Business Review* (Scott Berinato 2010).

Because we absorb more from success than failure, we can use positive feedback to improve our motivation and strengthen the neural connections (synapses) that lead toward our goals.

Challenge Your Mindset

Your brain is designed to make your life easier and comes with a particular function called automation. These shortcuts are built by the brain to help you respond fast to everyday activities, which is crucial in a high-demand world like ours.

It's a great feature—otherwise, you'd need to learn how to drive a car every time you sit in front of the wheel. However, it may become a flaw that creates a loop in your brain that repeats over and over again if you don't know how to deactivate it.

You may find it almost impossible when you try to change your conduct, a habit, or an already automated way of being. Your neurons try to travel the same old road again, no matter how hard you try to change it.

To change, you'll need to challenge your brain, stop believing everything it says to you, and start creating a growth mindset. The Brain Initiative program under the National Institutes of Health has shared significant discoveries about how the human brain contributes to our success[35]. They have found

---

[35] The Brain Research Through Advancing Innovative Neurotechnologies® (BRAIN) Initiative was launched in April 2013 by Barack Obama. A bold, new initiative aimed at revolutionizing our understanding of the human brain. To know more, visit https://braininitiative.nih.gov/. Two different teams of BRAIN Initiative-supported scientist—led by Arnold Kriegstein of the University of California and Stephen Smith of the University of Oxford—explains findings linking brain connectivity to measures of personal success (2015).

that part of the secret of the most successful people is that they are open to new ways of thinking and accept new perspectives. Consequently, their brain activity doesn't remain the same; critical parts of their brain connect in new and different ways. "The more successful we tend to be—score higher on commonly considered positive personal qualities, such as education and income levels and life satisfaction—the more key parts of our brain tend to talk to each other when we're not doing anything in particular.[36]"

Inside you, there's a marvelous being of light filled with endless potential. All you need to do is, as my guru said, improve your knowledge through meditation, brain reprogramming, and other powerful techniques. When used profoundly and holistically, lasting changes come most naturally.

> I am larger, better than I thought,
> I did not know I held so much goodness.
>
> —Walt Whitman

---

[36] Jules Asher 2015.

Being smart is not everything

Mute your inner saboteur

"I just don't know how to get the job I want; what am I doing wrong?"
"I'm not sure I have what it takes to land a better position."
"They are so senior and experienced; I don't think I'll measure up."
"If I try to go after a more fulfilling role, I'll let my family down."
"I'm not ready for this kind of challenge."
"My lack of confidence always betrays me."
"Is this the right time? What if I screw it up?"

This chapter is for you if you've ever asked yourself any of these questions at any point in your executive career.

Finding Executive Success Isn't Guesswork

Whether you aim to reach a higher job, succeed in your current role, change career paths, grow a new business, or get hired in a high-level executive position, you can find the success you're looking for. Strengthening your career strategy and perspective is crucial, and it will unleash and capitalize on all your experience and preparation.

Harnessing all your career potential means easing many aspects of the complex executive and professional game. You must pay attention to my five-step methodology to a career and life worth living to do this successfully.[37] However, it will mainly require you to master all career blocks you face, especially those inside you.

Those questions and many others come from a deep place inside you. It's an inner voice that seems to prevent something wrong, or even terrible, from happening. However, it's actually here to keep you where you are, specifically when there's a calling inside you to look out for more.

Only with an integral perspective that includes having the most powerful strategies and working with this inner voice will you be able to transform your career once and for all, and secure a meaningful job that you love and that gives you everything you've ever wanted.

This voice inside you is your inner saboteur, and it's like living with a neurotic roomie inside your head, as Brother Santoshananda—a Self-Realization Fellowship monk—said once.

Three Facts to Mute Your Inner Saboteur

1. Understand you are wired that way

According to the National Science Foundation, the average person has about 12,000 to 60,000 thoughts per day. The worst part is that 80 percent of this talk is negative feedback about ourselves: fears, doubts, insecurities, and criticism, among many others. 95% are exactly the same repetitive thoughts as the day before, and about 80% are negative (Simone 2017).

As Rick Hanson—senior fellow at UC Berkeley's Great Good Science Center—explains, your beautiful modern body contains a primitive brain that controls your innate and automatic self-preserving behavior patterns,

---

[37] To learn more, refer to Chapter 4 in Part III.

ensuring survival.[38] It means that "your brain is built more for avoiding than for approaching [pleasant experiences]. That's because it's the negative experiences, not the positive ones, that have generally had the most impact on survival" (Hanson 2009, 40).

Why would you need to know this to improve your professional and life experience? Every time you try to achieve something more meaningful for yourself or any gratification outside your brain's boundaries to preserve stability, your brain will freak out. That stability centers around a "good set-point and within certain ranges—not too hot, not too cold" (Hanson 2009, 32). It will find any deviation as a threat, even if it's good for you, e.g., more money, pleasure, fun, status, and so on.

Its natural mechanisms, specialized in detecting negative information faster than positive news, send an alarm that paralyzes your prefrontal cortex. This is the part of your brain that allows you to plan, think, and anticipate—in other words, that makes you the modern human you are.

If sometimes you feel lost and lonely with this loud voice (your neurotic roomie), join the club! We all feel the same.

The good news is that you will discover a proven and effective system to help you master this powerful voice and prevent him from blocking your career.

2. Dismantle his toolkit

A few days ago, one of my clients in Brazil (a country president at a large pharmaceutical company) was amazed at how dealing effectively with his saboteur has been key to competing successfully in three different processes for higher-level positions. One was in his company for a global role and two were with other Fortune 100 companies.

---

[38] The hindbrain is the most primitive of the central nervous system (CNS) regions. The cerebellum and lower brain stem structures, the medulla, and the pons are located in this division. It's what most neuroscientists call the proto reptilian brain. In MacLean's triune brain model, the basal ganglia are referred to as the reptilian or primal brain (Hanson 2009).

It would be very convenient to apply a one-size-fits-all formula to tame this annoying neurotic roomie. Still, the truth is that it will take time and patience to listen to what he is saying, note the correlated emotions, and ease the rush.

Most times, it requires expert help to unmask the saboteur's repertoire due to the breadth and depth of his toolkit. Here are four clues you can start using right away to take the first step.

1. Write down everything he tells you

2. Identify the emotions that arise in you with each of his statements.

3. Try to identify patterns.

I'm aware it may be like rocket science, and it's tough to work it ourselves. It would require a considerable capacity to watch over our own mental, emotional, and psychological traits and states.[39]

Once you've dismantled him, you'll find your way free of most of the blockers you've ever experienced.

3. Transform him into an ally

Most people don't know that their inner saboteur has impressive power. That is why you can't fight it back. It's here to stay and to fight the battle until the end, though it will come with high costs for you, your career, and your life.

It's not always easy to measure all the costs and the opportunities you've missed because your grouchy inner roomie is sabotaging you and reminding you every time about all your shortfalls and lacks.

---

[39] It reminds me of an extreme case portrayed in the movie *A Beautiful Mind*. Russell Crowe plays a brilliant professor who, at a certain point, becomes aware of his own schizophrenia. Of course, it's a movie, but it would be great to have that power, even though we're lucky not to be schizophrenics.

A good exercise is to list everything you've lost because of him. This will also help you understand how he works. At first, it may appear like a voice trying to protect you from losing something vital for you or to alert you to danger. But his true nature is to hold you back and keep you where you are, especially when you take risks to reach a better life and career.

Now that you're aware, the real question is what can you do about him?

When we repeatedly have the same thoughts, something happens inside our brains: neurons create long-term relationships. "Neurons that fire together, wire together," as neuroscientist Donald Hebb said, and this long-time memory makes changing so challenging. Any experience, emotion, or situation like the one that triggers your thoughts will activate this synapsis.

Dealing with your inner saboteur effectively and permanently requires changing your thoughts and beliefs so profoundly that it will rewire your brain and create new synapses. This will help you grow instead of block your career. Don't buy into everything he tells you.

Every thought you have is the perfect opportunity to transform your saboteur into an ally.

> Sometimes people need to lie to themselves most of all.
>
> —Patrick Ness

Part VII

Break free to love yourself and life fully

I am not my thoughts, emotions, sense perceptions,
and experiences. I am not the content of my life.
I am life. I am the space in which all things happen.
I am consciousness. I am the Now. I am.

—Eckhart Tolle

When the "perfect job" is not enough

It sounds crazy, right? When so many people struggle to get a good job, the "perfect job" has become a privilege. Without a doubt, it is. Why is it so difficult to enjoy it, to make the journey an adventure that stimulates and brings out the best in us?

The truth is no one has ever taught us to do it. On the contrary, we live in a world that tells us that only with great efforts can we stand out and be successful. They have even said to us that work is so terrible that they even pay us to do it, right?

I've worked so hard, and I can't get "there."

Want to Jump off the Window?

Wait. Not yet. The latest science shows us otherwise.

That's why I thought I'd share with you some ideas that can help you have a different perspective on work. Changing your perspective can help you transform work into an experience that, far from generating so much stress, wear, and exhaustion, can be satisfying, motivating, and even amusing.

If you are tired of chronic exhaustion, gastritis, insomnia, weekends connected to email, tics, dark circles, lack of energy, or any other symptom of burnout, or if you know someone like that, this is for you. Maybe here you will find some valuable ideas.

Where the @*%$!*# is My Happiness?

Many professionals and executives come to me with all kinds of goals, challenges, and problems. Among all of them, two types are very relevant to this topic.

1 Want to get their perfect job	Most people are looking to find more enticing professional opportunities. That may mean many different things to everyone: promotions to higher positions, changing companies or areas, changing career paths, feeling fully alive and enthusiastic about their jobs, starting side businesses or start-ups, leaving marks that make them feel proud, going back to corporate business, or breaking free from corporate companies. In short, there are many reasons, but most want something better, more fulfilling, and rewarding –by all means.
2 Want to get rid of their perfect job	Surprising as it may sound, a group of people seem to have everything any professional would aspire to, yet they're not happy. It takes courage to recognize we're here. When we do, there's no limit to what we can achieve using the platforms we have already created.

I've written this chapter for all those souls who are yearning for something else. And I'm here to share great news: it's possible to attain everlasting happiness, fulfillment, and joy. That's what we're here for, after all.

First, we may want to know that this situation is far more common than we think. Moreover, I would say that it's "natural" and universal, part of our human essence, even though we all express it in different ways, moments, and intensities.

Science explains why (as we'll see later) and confirms what the ancient spiritual teachers have taught for eons.[40]

They have "perfect jobs": high executive positions in top global companies. They have high, even extraordinary, incomes, including admiringly competitive salaries, bonuses, company cars, and all kinds of flex benefits and exec perquisites. They enjoy business-class world traveling. Everything seems just perfect. Everyone admires them and looks for their support and approval.

On the inside, however, daily struggles continue. One way or another, they can't manage to let things flow smoothly and to let themselves breathe and enjoy.

They can't easily face all the high-complexity challenges of their roles: political issues, punchy leadership styles, unfair peer competition, conflicting objectives, hidden agendas, difficult colleagues, and slight yet painful differences in salaries and compensation, among many others. The list might be endless, as they are highly demanding organizations and roles.

Other times, they just can't find the time, energy, and balance to enjoy what they have and are creating, or they do not manage to feel completely fulfilled and happy.

---

[40] Jesus Christ, Buddha, Krishna, and all the illuminated souls have taught that the way to attain everlasting joy, peace, and happiness lies within us. Buddha said, "Happiness lies within. It is useless to seek it elsewhere." People usually ask me about my own path; for over three decades, I've followed a soul-liberating path by the hand of an enlightened guru, Paramahansa Yogananda. If your soul is also yearning for a more profound and joyful life experience, you can learn more here: www.yogananda-srf.org

One More Confession

(Gosh, is she ever gonna stop confessing?)

I went through it myself. I had opened a magnificent career path. I was already enjoying regional, global, and national achievements, which came with all the means of the world's more giant corporations: multiple business-class trips, international meetings, world awards, and all the Fortune 100 glamour.

I felt weird when I found it bored me very quickly, and I couldn't find it attractive anymore. To be honest, it filled me with some mild guilt. I thought there was something wrong with me. Maybe I was depressed?

As an expert in human and executive development, I knew perfectly well that I should be grateful for all that. Don't get me wrong: I was very grateful. However, I deeply yearned for something more. As a highly trained psychologist, I also knew I wasn't depressed, but longed for something "real and genuine."

Despite my great horizons and the career path in front of me, I decided to quit my executive career. To everybody's surprise, I left and never came back.

I read tons of books and did a lot of internal work. My years of dedication and study included training as an executive and career coach in the United Kingdom and San Diego, participating in global and regional teams creating talent development programs, launching several corporate universities, training in sales and marketing in San Diego, and studying for an MBA. Finally, I managed to create a complete, fulfilling professional life for myself. It took me many more years than I would have liked, but I did it.

Now I live a life full of everything I love. Furthermore, I dedicate myself to helping others achieve this goal—whatever it may mean for them—much easier and faster, without all the effort it involved for me.

You don't have to invest so much time, energy, and effort. You don't have to be kamikaze. Here are all the shortcuts. If you apply even a tiny percentage of everything I'm sharing with you in this book and in my programs, you'll change your job and life forever. All my coachees and students know the power of these strategies and tools.

You would be surprised by the number of executives in this scenario who come to me for advice on achieving more satisfying and enjoyable professional lives.

They work for the most valued luxury car companies, in the most avant-garde pharma companies, in the most dynamic consumer products corporations—in short, in all kinds of large companies that are distinguished by taking care of talent and retaining it. Nevertheless, they look to me because they often feel unhappy, unrecognized, and wasted. They ask me for help to "find meaning," "have true experiences," "be seen for what they are," and "feel passionate about what they do again." In short, they want to straighten something that at some point was diverted, twisted, or definitely lost.

How could someone feel unhappy or overwhelmed if he or she leads the world? How could someone feel unhappy or overwhelmed if he or she works in the best environment with all the amenities of post-pandemic life? How could someone feel unhappy or overwhelmed if he or she lives in a penthouse with a spectacular view of the skyline of the most beautiful metropolis? It's absurd, right? No way.

What happened?

The Delusion of Success and Happiness

In the globalized world, overly demanding and saturated with stimuli and information, in which we live, with increasingly stretched goals, more appealing options, and higher levels of well-being, people are subject to exponential pressures. The competition has become almost unbearable at work and in our personal lives.

Just take a look at any of your social networks. Everyone seems to have an enviable life: traveling all the time to the best places in the world, enjoying great and fun relationships, and living extraordinary and meaningful experiences day after day. All of this funded by a fantastic part-time job so flexible and generous that it allows any exotic excursion of more than six months to the most remote place on the planet.

Of course, we all want to get there.

The thing is that all this puts a lot of weight on us. Have you felt it? On the one hand, there is the overdemand of the wonderful world; on the other, there is the feared freefall into oblivion. However, there are two big problems:

1. **Social media sells a false reality.**

    Life is different, and you know it unless you are one of the heirs to the eight wealthiest families in the world—even Musk, Zuckerberg, and Bezos meet difficulties. Although we know this rationally, we feel compelled to cover unrealistic and irrational expectations while facing the challenges and situations of our realities. We all get sick and sad and face diverse problems, complex relations, and other challenges.

    In the midst of all this, what remains are ourselves and our dreams, concerns, desires, efforts, talents, potential, and above all, our ability to transform our realities, create what we truly want, and make ourselves happy.

    Not all happiness and wellness is everlasting.

    Shine will diminish as soon as we get what we want.

    According to Rick Hanson, because of our brain design, reaching for pleasure can also make us suffer from the following:

    - Desire itself can be unpleasant, and even mild longing is subtly uncomfortable.
    - When you fulfill a desire, the rewards that follow are not often as great.
    - When rewards are, in fact, pretty great, many of them still come at a stiff price.

- Even if you do what you want, it's genuinely great, and it doesn't cost much—the gold standard—every pleasant experience must inevitably change and end (Hanson 2009, 39).

What if, however, you could defy all this and find everlasting happiness?

Scientific Brain Facts: Beating Paradigms

It blew my mind when I discovered the science of happiness and positive psychology. Researchers such as Tal Ben-Shahar, Sonja Lyubomisrky, and Mihaly Csikszentmihalyi tell us we can pursue everlasting joy and happiness, can show us the way, and can confirm what the illuminated teachers have told us over millennia.

What really happens when you get the "perfect job," and indeed, given everything we're talking about, it's not enough or it doesn't make you happy?

Many factors influence, correct? These include workload, pressures, corporate politics, and so on. What if you could modulate them to enjoy and face challenges from a place of greater peace of mind without all the sweat and tears?

In fact, it's doable.

Science has shown that the outside world can only predict 10 percent of your long-term happiness and success, and the other 90 percent comes from how you process that outer experiences (Achor n.d.). Living under the traditional paradigm that declares that fulfillment comes from outside is the perfect recipe for frustration and burnout.

Does this mean that we should become Tibetan monks? Should we leave everything material and not pursue any goals? No way. It means that the way I signify what happens to me is as important, or more so, than the events themselves. From there, I will react and create a reality for myself. To the extent that I positively symbolize events and live, as I say, in learning mode, I will make a positive, easy reality and a more enjoyable experience.

Be careful, because this has nothing to do with the magical thinking that states I'll command the world, and it will obey me just because I said so. No. It has to do with the fact that my interpretation of the facts generates thoughts that create chemical responses in my brain and body. Later, they are transformed into reactions, attitudes, and responses toward the outside, which, in turn, respond accordingly—it is that easy.

As one of the prominent minds in this field said,

> Happiness is not something that happens. It is not the result of good luck or chance. It is not something that can be bought with money or power. It does not seem to depend on external events, but rather on how we interpret them.
>
> —Mihaly Csikszentmihalyi[41]

Another usual paradigm is "happy ever after," as in the movies. We believe that because we have already reached a goal, we are already on the other side, and now we'll be happy forever. Nothing could be more unreal.

Research shows that our brains are designed to forget. Blake Richards and Paul Frankland at the University of Toronto have found "there are mechanisms that promote memory loss."[42] That is why after just two weeks of achieving a goal, we completely forget about the sense of accomplishment and privilege. We focus only on the burden, the competition, the responsibilities, the difficulties, the pressure, complaints, deadlines, and new startlines.

Again, does this mean it is not worth setting goals and striving for them? On the contrary, the point is letting go of unrealistic expectations that tell us we'll be safe after arrival, which will solve everything. We had better learn to enjoy the journey, with all the benefits, ups and downs, and challenges it implies.

Experts have found that IQ predicts only 25 percent of success; the remaining 75 percent comes from our levels of optimism, our abilities to perceive stress as a challenge not as a threat, and from social support networks and effective networking (Achor n.d.).

---

[41] Csikszentmihalyi 2004.
[42] Campbell 2017.

In addition, neuroscience shows us that every time we reach a goal, our brains not only set new, more ambitious goals, as might be expected. They also reframe the very meaning and sense of success. If happiness is on the other side of success, our brains never get there.

"We have pushed happiness beyond the cognitive horizon" (Achor et al. 2011). We have sent happiness to an inaccessible place for our brains. Naturally, we are overwhelmed, overpowered, and unable to enjoy what we do and what we have.

So, Which Way?

Here is the good news (and I love that).

Once we start understanding all these brain mechanisms, we begin to see the light.

It is not only necessary to reduce our stress and increase our job satisfaction to have better health, balance, and well-being, but it also has a considerable impact on productivity.

When we raise our levels of optimism, our brains work significantly better: intelligence, creativity, and energy levels rise, and therefore, our career and life prospects improve. Specialists call this effect the happiness advantage (Achor 2010).

The positive brain is 31 percent more productive. It generates a substantial decrease in burnout, and resilience increases. As you know, we emerge stronger from adverse experiences; we are 37 percent more effective, 19 percent faster, and more accurate (Lyubomirsky 2005).

All this also makes sense at the level of brain chemistry. When we have positive brains, we secrete dopamine, which not only makes us feel happier but activates all the learning centers in the brain, allowing us to adapt to the world differently.

If you want a better balance, a better career, higher ROI in your professional efforts, and therefore higher bonuses without so much attrition, you need to change how you see things. You need to learn to have a new perspective that favors your adaptation, flexibility, learning, and, in the end, your ability to respond optimally. Consequently, you create a better reality for yourself and those close to you: your team, your family, your bosses, even the company itself.

Simple, Clever Changes

Getting there requires implementing some effortless changes that support life balance and positive thinking.

The first fight you'll have to fight before implementing them will be with your brain. It will tell you that all this is ridiculous nonsense. How could such easy actions change your life?

Well, that part of your brain speaking is the automation function. It's designed to do the same things the same way over and over again to make life easier for you. It is the part that allows you to drive your car without thinking about what movement is next so you save time and energy.

You'll have to negotiate with that party to be able to execute any of these easy-to-implement actions. If you succeed, you will see how your perspective changes and, therefore, your life. You will tell me how everything changed for you.

There are many ways to train your brain to be more positive and productive and help you achieve your career, balance, and life goals.

You only need to practice them for two minutes for twenty-one consecutive days, and you can begin to rewire and retrain your brain.

1. Redirect your thoughts. Whenever you have a negative view, about yourself, anyone, or anything, focus on the opposite quality.

2. Practice unconditional gratitude. It's easy to be thankful for the good things. When you are thankful for the bad things, you let them go and free your emotions to refocus your brain on the positive.
3. Meditate. It will help you find an inner place of calm. As Paramahansa Yogananda said, "You realize that all along there was something tremendous within you, and you did not know it" (Self-Realization Fellowship Site)[43].
4. Practice middle-intensity exercises. You will secrete as many endorphins as eating chocolate, with a perdurable effect.
5. Keep a gratitude and learning journal. Write daily about your positive experiences and what you have learned, and be thankful for the hard ones.
6. Practice mindfulness. Focusing on the present moment will enrich your daily experience and give you a new balance. As Brother Satyananda has said, "Be here now, be somewhere else later" (Self-Realization World Convocation 2015)[44].
7. Engage in outdoor activities. Any contact with nature will nurture your spirit and help you find more balance and natural fulfillment.

Something additional that I recommend to my coachees is to live in a criticism-free zone. It is a straightforward concept, and it only requires the discipline to avoid any negative comments throughout the day, including those directed against me. Now that I'm writing it, I'm going to add living in a violence-free zone too.

---

[43] Meditating is not blanking your mind, as many people think, but immersing yourself in an experience of peace, love, and joy. There are advanced techniques that will help you achieve this experience faster. For guided meditation, go to www.yogananda.org/guided-meditations.
[44] As a monk of Paramahansa Yogananda's Self-Realization Fellowship (SRF) monastic community for over forty years, Brother Satyananda has inspired audiences in North and South America, Europe, Australia, and New Zealand with his dynamic presentations on the ancient philosophy of yoga and time-honored science of meditation. Presently he resides at the Self-Realization Fellowship Lake Shrine in Pacific Palisades, California, where he serves as minister in charge. Brother Satyananda, whose name denotes "the attainment of bliss through the truth," was born in San Diego, California. To watch his talk on "Renewing Our Spiritual Enthusiasm," visit bit.ly/BroSatyanandaConvocation.

Attaining lasting happiness requires that we enjoy the journey on our way toward a destination we deem valuable. Happiness is not about making it to the peak of the mountain, nor is it about climbing aimlessly around the mountain; happiness is the experience of climbing toward the peak.

—Tal Ben-Shahar

Silent violence

The soul's murderer

A few days ago, I was talking to one of my clients, a senior commercial vice president for a large fast-moving consumer goods company in the United States. He shared how much easier it has been for him to face the waxes and wanes at his job since we began working together and how having an expert's insight has dramatically impacted his career. He made my day! This also made me think about how I've been able to help thousands of people and how I have achieved so many challenging goals for myself. Still, it was herculean to overcome a personal situation that I faced a few years ago that kept me imprisoned for longer than I've ever wanted.

We all know well that it's part of life to experience ups and downs, but sometimes we feel completely overwhelmed and hopeless when we're down. When we find ourselves in toxic relationships, in frontal or passive-aggressive environments, or in negative situations that drain our energy and break our dreams. We cannot find our way out until we find the right help and tools.

I was there. I remember how hard it was to try to keep a family, a couple's relationship, and my business afloat without any help from my partner. Don't get me wrong: he was there; he just didn't lift a finger. I was in a hyper-demanding and violent situation that was so sugarcoated, civilized, and subtle that it took me a while to realize what it was. It took even more time, effort, money, and energy to change and leave it behind.

I Was Enslaved Once

It's somehow easy to identify physical and verbal violence, but not so simple to move away from it. Still, some abusive behaviors are much more subtle and hard to see. This violence was pointed to as perverse by Marie-France Hirigoyen[45] in the broader connotation of the word (1998, 17). As psychologist Christian Mormont explains,

> From the clinical point of view, the perverse personality is characterized by constant manipulation of others, transgression of laws, and disrespect of limits. Perversity does not refer to the presence of a sexual perversion, whether primary or associated, but to the fact that the same basic principle underlies the organization of the perverse personality and the perverse sexuality. Both forms could thus be understood as two different manifestations of intolerance to disappointment. (Mormont 1990)

In short, it's about moral perversion. The perverse personality will try to benefit at the expense of others, to obtain satisfaction from inflicting suffering on someone else.

We face these personalities all the time, everywhere. This is the person who wants to take advantage, create conflict, and laugh when the scapegoat is singled out. At school, this is the schoolmate who did not participate in team projects and manipulated the situation to implicate at others. At work, these people constantly complain and underdeliver; they may seem super-busy doing nothing. When someone asks about their progress, they say they are almost done. They may wander the office with smiles and friendly attitudes, disqualifying, dividing, and criticizing those who work to, finally, try to reap

---

[45] Psychiatrist, psychoanalyst, and psychotherapist specializing in mobbing, a form of bullying, details in her book *Moral Harassment: the Perverse Violence in Everyday Life* all the traits of this kind of violence in private life (within couples and families) and at work.

what the others planted. While commuting, they hinder traffic due to their lack of civility and headshakes at others.

There are many manifestations, and most of them can be noticed. Any regular person can behave like that in a given moment. For instance, the person may rage then moves to a different behavior and questions himself or herself about what happened. It only becomes destructive with frequency and repetition.

The thing is that there's an even more subtle *modus operandi* that is hard to see and unveil. I've seen it widely in families and businesses through my own experience and the experiences of my coachees and students. This is the person who is enchanting but not contributing at all; someone others have to subsidize in every way because the person just can't give anything, even if he or she "tries hard." This person will not shout, humiliate, ridicule, or attack frontally. He or she will just sit back and see you die trying.

When we get into relationships with perverse people, the situations deteriorate in intangible and unsuspected ways. They are kind, lovely, and thankful, which will feed our egos. They will make us feel we are so generous and powerful to have rescued such a weak and incapable being. What would they be without us? What a mind game. They know they're abusing us, so we should not entertain any doubts here,[46] but they won't stop. They're enjoying themselves while receiving many privileges with no effort at all.

Every time I see a sign of this slavery, which they caught themselves in because of a need to be loved and to belong, in any of my coachees and clients, I work with it delicately and softly. It's quite painful. We prefer to maintain situations that drain us in many ways, to be silent and feed the lies for fear of pain. We choose to believe all the excuses and explanations before realizing someone who was supposed to love us and be there for us is hurting and abusing us.

Sometimes it happens at work, and we subsidize our colleagues or team. I've found that often, when it happens to us in one place, it most probably occurs

---

[46] I remember once my ex-partner's words about a passive president who was doing nothing for the country. He said, "You can do a lot of damage just by doing nothing."

in other arenas. Most of the time, that's why we're overloaded with work, burned out, and without balance. We deserve better than that.

Don't panic. There's a way out, and creating consciousness about it is the very first step. Trust me. If you identify with what I've described, you're not as powerless as you think, and the others will not die without you.[47]

I know it will take a while to understand this truth, but you will eventually. In my experience, how fortified and quickly we can put limits on ourselves and put ourselves in good shelters is impressive.

An exercise I like to use with my coachees, and myself, is this.

Imagine you're gone; how would they solve their situation? What would they do? Well, let them do exactly that starting now.

Here is an extra tip: feeling guilty when doing this exercise or feeling it's your responsibility to solve their problems are good signs that you may be experiencing the slavery I experienced once. But the imprisonment was my own mind and feelings, so there's always a way out.

I'm In Love

A couple of weeks ago, I found myself very much in love with life and everything I have created so far.

During this journey, I've learned that if there is anything inside me that screams or whispers to move on to a better life, at work or personally, it's vital to listen to it. After all, it's my life, and I really want it to be as awesome as it can be.

If you've ever felt the same way about something in your life or work, you might want to give it a try. It may not be that dramatic. Maybe it's something subtle, or something that's holding you back from unleashing the fullness of

---

[47] You're not alone. I want you to know that if you identify with any of these, I'm here for you. Email me, and I'll love to help you set yourself free. We'll figure it out. talktoyardena@careerenlightenacademy.com. You can also visit my specialized site: www.happinesspathways.com.

your life. Perhaps you don't even know what to do about it; it's okay. What matters is how amazing you want your work and life to be. It is worthy, you are worthy, and it is possible.

That's why it's so vital for me to help other people. Even when you are not experiencing something as dramatic, the longing for something better can be subtly painful. You deserve to live your life at the top, to reach the job you want that will give you all the fulfillment, reward, recognition, balance, fun, financial security, and whatever else will make you feel completely alive.

Empower your career and life dreams

> When you can touch someone's heart...
> that's limitless.
>
> —Steve Jobs

Those were the beautiful words that Steve Jobs spoke at the Apple Town Hall, that mythical staff meeting in which he presented the first iPod to his entire team in 2001. With it, he transformed the world.

Before Jobs, it would have been unthinkable to hear something like that from a businessperson, right?

What impact did that have? How did he lead Apple to become the most relevant technology company of all time, and what does it have to do with you? Will it be possible to use this connection and this spirit to take your career to new heights and accelerate the achievement of your goals?

The Evidence

It's been twenty years since that historic moment in 2001, and these are Apple's results since then.

According to Statista, in 2005, Apple's net income amounted to 1.33 billion dollars; by the end of 2021, it recorded 94.68 billion dollars. In the last sixteen years, it has grown more than seventy times. It is as if someone who earns a hundred thousand dollars a month ends up making 7 million dollars a month. That exponential growth is unprecedented (Laricchia 2022).

Apply It to Your Career

Part of the secret to this impressive success is that when we have a dream and put our hearts into making it happen, something magical happens, and we move the universe.

Of course, that implies work—often, a lot of work—talent, dedication, effort, and more, without a doubt. How many times do we invest enormous amounts of work and effort without being able to achieve what we want? Has it happened to you?

It certainly happened to me, as you have read. It was very frustrating, and it wasn't until I learned to take action intelligently and use this kind of strength and energy that I achieved a growth spurt. Today, I feel deeply grateful for it. And I want to invite you to accelerate your goals too. Are you ready?

Think About What Your Dream Is Today

Forget whether or not you can achieve it, your doubts, and what you think it may involve.

Just let yourself be carried away by it. Close your eyes for a moment and imagine yourself there. It doesn't matter how you got there, but you're already there.

Feel your heart; how does it feel? Do you feel happy or joyful? Are you smiling or singing? Let yourself be there with her. She's your future's self heart, and you're connecting with her now. Don't let your doubts take you away from her. Hug her, squeeze her to your chest, and tell her that you are here for her, just as she is for you. Tell her that you are finally in the right place to make it happen. Thank her for waiting for you and not quitting on you. Tell her that you will do whatever it takes to achieve your dream.

Take the First Step

Don't let anything or anyone stop you, and do not worry about how to make it happen. That's why we're here. Let me guide you. I know the path; I've walked it. I've accompanied so many people on this journey that I can tell you, without fear of being wrong, that it is possible to walk it successfully. There are strategies and tools to progress with more speed, security, certainty, and confidence more easily and faster than you imagine.

> The question isn't who is going to let me.
> It's who is going to stop me.
>
> —Ayn Rand

And soon, you will awaken and say, "wherever I look, behind the path I've traveled and shining on every stone as I step forward, there is light, lots of light!"

References

Achor, Shawn. 2010. "The Happiness Advantage: How a Positive Brain Fuels Success in Work and Life." New York: Penguin Random House.

Achor, Shawn. n.d. "The Happy Secret to Better Work." Harvard Business Review. Filmed at TEDxBloomington. Video, 12:04. https://www.ted.com/talks/shawn_achor_the_happy_secret_to_better_work/

Achor, Shawn, Andrew Reece, Gabriella Rosen Kellerman, and Alexi Robichaux. 2018. "9 Out of 10 People Are Willing to Earn Less Money to Do More-Meaningful Work." *Harvard Business Review*. Posted November 6, 2018. https://hbr.org/2018/11/9-out-of-10-people-are-willing-to-earn-less-money-to-do-more-meaningful-work.

Asher, Donald. 2007. *Who Gets Promoted, Who Doesn't, and Why: 10 Things You'd Better Do if You Want to Get Ahead*. New York: Ten Speed Press.

Asher, Jules. 2015. Our brain's secrets to success? *National Institutes of Health*. Posted September 28, 2015. https://www.nih.gov/news-events/news-releases/our-brains-secrets-success.

Ben-Shahar, Tal. 2007. *Happier: Learn the Secrets to Daily Joy and Lasting Fulfillment*. New York: McGraw-Hill.

Berinato, Scott. 2010. "Success Gets into Your Head and Changes It." *Harvard Business Review*. From the Magazine January-February, 2010. https://hbr.org/2010/01/success-gets-into-your-head-and-changes-it.

Bradt, Steve. 2010. "Wandering mind not a happy mind." *The Harvard Gazette*. Posted November 11, 2010. https://news.harvard.edu/gazette/story/2010/11/wandering-mind-not-a-happy-mind/.

Buckingham, Marcus, and Donald O. Clifton. 2001. *Now, Discover Your Strengths: How to Develop Your Talents and Those of the People You Manage.* New York: Free Press.

Buckingham, Marcus. 2022. *Love and Work: How To Find What You Love, Love What You Do, and Do It for the Rest of Your Life.* Boston, MA: Harvard Business School Publishing.

Campbell, Don. 2017. "Why Forgetting is Really Important For Memory: U of T Research." University of Toronto Site. Posted June 21, 2017. https://www.utoronto.ca/news/why-forgetting-really-important-memory- u-t-research.

Cotteleer, Mark and Sniderman, Brenna. 2017. "Forces of change: Industry 4.0." *Deloitte Site.* Posted December 18, 2017. https://www2.deloitte.com/us/en/insights/focus/industry-4-0/overview.html.

Csikszentmihalyi, Mihaly. 2004. *Good Business: Leadership, Flow, and the Making of Meaning.* New York: Penguin.

Degenhard, J. 2021. "Forecast of the number of LinkedIn users in the World from 2017 to 2025." *Statista Site.* Posted July 20, 2021.https://www.statista.com/forecasts/1147197/linkedin-users-in-the-world.

Dispenza, Joe. 2013. *Breaking The Habit of Being Yourself: How to Lose Your Mind and Create a New One.* Carlsbad, CA: Hay House Inc.

Dixon, S. 2022. "Leading countries based on LinkedIn audience size as of April 2022." *Statista Site.* Posted July 27, 2022. https://www.statista.com/statistics/272783/linkedins-membership-worldwide-by-country/.

El Financiero Site. 2019. "3 CEO Mexicanas te Dicen Cómo Romper el Techo de Cristal." Posted June 13, 2019. https://www.elfinanciero.com.mx/empresas/3-ceo-mexicanas-te-dicen-como-se-rompe-el-techo-de-cristal/.

Hanson, Rick. 2009. *Buddha's Brain: The Practical Neuroscience of Happiness, Love, and Wisdom.* Oakland, CA: New Harbinger.

Hendricks, Gay. 2009. *The Big Leap: Conquer Your Hidden Fear and Take Life to the Next Level.* New York: HarperOne.

Hirigoyen, Marie-France. 1998. *Le Harcèlement Moral: La Violence Perverse Au Quotidien.* Paris: La Dècouverte y Syros.

Laricchia, Federica. 2022. "Apple's Net Income in the Company's Fiscal Years From 2005 to 2021." *Statista Site*. Posted July 27, 2022. https://www.statista.com/statistics/267728/apples-net-income-since-2005/.

Mormont, C. 1990. "The Perverse Personality." *National Library of Medicine* 1990;90(5-6):278-88. https://pubmed.ncbi.nlm.nih.gov/1670404/.

Salary Site. 2013. "Salary Negotiation: Separating Fact from Fiction." Posted September 23, 2013. https://www.salary.com/chronicles/salary-negotiation-separating-fact-from-fiction/.

Segall, Laurie. 2013. "Steve Jobs' Last Gift." *CNN Business*. Posted September 10, 2013. https://money.cnn.com/2013/09/10/technology/steve-jobs-gift/index.html#:~:text=One%20of%20Steve%20Jobs'%20last,by%20Hindu%20guru%20Paramahansa%20Yogananda.

Self-Realization Fellowship Site. n.d. "Self-Realization Fellowship. Founded 1920 by Paramahansa Yogananda." https://yogananda.org/.

Simone, Fran. 2017. "Negative Self-Talk: Don't Let It Overwhelm You." *Psychology Today*. Posted December 4, 2017. https://www.psychologytoday.com/ca/blog/family-affair/201712/negative-self-talk-dont-let-it-overwhelm-you.

World Economic Forum Site. 2016. "Brain Plasticity Explained: Yes, You Really Can Change Your Brain." Posted October 3, 2016. https://www.weforum.org/agenda/2016/10/brain-plasticity-yes-you-really-can-change-your-brain/.

Yogananda Site. 2016. "A Spiritual Tribute to George Harrison—Beatle and Devotee of Yoganada." Posted November 24, 2016. https://yoganandasite.wordpress.com/2016/11/24/a-spiritual-tribute-to-george-harrison-beatle-and-devotee-of-yogananda/.

Index

A

Achievements 16, 50, 54, 55, 65, 75, 77, 78, 95, 107, 124, 138
Assertive communication 63

B

Beliefs 20, 21, 22, 36, 86, 115
Ben-Shahar, Tal 77, 127, 132, 141
Brain 22, 33, 35, 37, 38, 39, 40, 42, 44, 47, 49, 90, 107, 108, 109, 110, 112, 113, 115, 126, 127, 128, 129, 130, 131, 141, 142, 143
    Brain plasticity 38, 143
    programming 107

C

Career v, vi, vii, xi, xv, 5, 8, 9, 16, 17, 18, 20, 21, 23, 24, 25, 33, 35, 36, 40, 47, 48, 49, 52, 53, 54, 61, 62, 63, 72, 73, 77, 79, 87, 89, 91, 92, 94, 95, 103, 104, 105, 106, 107, 108, 111, 112, 113, 114, 115, 122, 124, 129, 130, 133, 138, 139
    Career Growth 77, 95
    Career Strategy vii, xi, xiii, 5, 8, 9, 18, 21, 24, 25, 26, 33, 35, 41, 42, 48, 49, 53, 54, 56, 57, 61, 62, 63, 66, 70, 72, 75, 76, 77, 78, 88, 89, 91, 92, 106, 108, 111, 112, 125, 140
Change v, 3, 7, 8, 9, 16, 19, 22, 24, 38, 48, 86, 93, 103, 108, 109, 110, 111, 125, 127, 130, 134, 141, 142, 143
Coaching v, vi, 17, 20, 59, 61, 69
Colleagues 6, 26, 45, 49, 72, 74, 103, 123, 135
Compensation 88, 89, 123
Confidence 18, 20, 21, 25, 36, 90, 111, 140
Csikszentmihalyi, Mihaly 77, 127, 128, 142
CV 44, 53, 69, 70, 73, 74, 75, 80
    main three pitfalls 70, 74

D

Delusion 19, 125
Disappointment 134
Doubts 6, 9, 28, 42, 79, 80, 85, 90, 112, 121, 135, 139
Dreams v, vi, vii, 5, 6, 17, 25, 26, 71, 95, 102, 126, 133, 138, 139, 140

E

Einstein, Albert 85
Emotional intelligence 36, 73, 78

Emotions 21, 28, 38, 86, 88, 114, 115, 119, 131
Energy 8, 17, 19, 21, 25, 26, 27, 102, 122, 123, 124, 129, 130, 133, 134, 139
Enthusiasm 8, 26, 131
Executive v, vi, vii, xiii, 5, 6, 9, 16, 17, 20, 24, 35, 39, 41, 42, 44, 48, 52, 53, 54, 55, 56, 61, 62, 64, 66, 67, 69, 70, 71, 74, 77, 78, 87, 88, 89, 90, 91, 92, 93, 94, 95, 101, 103, 104, 105, 111, 112, 122, 123, 124, 125
    Executive positioning 54, 55
    Executive positions 55, 111, 123
Exposure 53, 92

F

Fear 9, 21, 28, 86, 112, 135, 140, 142
Financial 15, 21, 23, 24, 33, 47, 49, 85, 86, 90, 94, 137
    Financial freedom 15, 33, 86, 90
    Financial goals 21
    Financial position 24
    Financial pressures 47
    Financial security 137
    Financial stability 94
Five enlightening questions 18, 19, 24
Five-step methodology 35, 112
Freedom 15, 17, 22, 33, 86, 90
    Freedom, financial 15, 33, 86, 90
Fulfillment 11, 72, 123, 127, 131, 137, 141

G

Gates, Bill 107
Genius 44, 47, 96
Goals
    Goals, life 5, 16, 17, 18, 21, 23, 24, 25, 28, 33, 35, 62, 65, 70, 73, 103, 104, 105, 106, 109, 122, 124, 125, 127, 128, 129, 130, 133, 138, 139
    Goals, career 17, 73, 106
    Goals, financial 21
Gratifications 49, 51, 113
Gratitude 9, 131
Growth vii, xv, 21, 24, 25, 36, 39, 56, 66, 72, 74, 75, 77, 87, 92, 95, 107, 108, 109, 139

H

Hanson, Rick 112, 126, 142
Happiness 21, 22, 72, 122, 123, 125, 126, 127, 128, 129, 132, 141, 142
Headhunter xi, 64, 69, 70, 79, 87, 89, 94
    Hunting 47, 68
Helpline 63
Hiring Manager 36, 55, 56, 63, 69, 70, 71, 94
Human Resources (HR) vi, xiii, 7, 66, 69, 70, 87, 88, 89, 91

I

Inner saboteur 111, 112, 114, 115
Inspiration xv, 10, 51
Interviews 7, 8, 35, 49, 53, 54, 64, 71, 76, 77, 78, 79, 88, 90, 94, 107, 108
    Interviews – unbeatable formula 79

J

Jesus Christ 123
Job vi, xiii, 5, 6, 7, 8, 9, 10, 15, 16, 17, 18, 20, 24, 25, 26, 27, 28, 33, 35, 36, 41, 44, 45, 46, 48, 54, 56, 63, 65, 66, 67, 68, 70, 71, 72, 74, 76, 77, 78, 79, 87, 88, 101, 103, 105, 108, 111, 112, 121, 122, 123, 125, 127, 129, 133, 137, 138, 143
    Job-getting commercial 56, 63, 66, 67

Job, perfect job 5, 35, 70, 121, 122, 123, 127
Jobs, Steve 10, 138, 143

K

Krishna, Lord 123

L

Learning v, 24, 48, 49, 51, 107, 127, 129, 130, 131
Lifestyle xiii, 6, 24, 41, 87, 94
Life worth living 35, 112
LinkedIn vi, 35, 42, 69, 71, 72, 73, 92, 94, 108, 142
Love xv, 5, 8, 15, 17, 20, 21, 24, 27, 49, 50, 96, 104, 107, 112, 117, 124, 129, 131, 135, 136, 142

M

Market xi, 7, 28, 54, 65, 66, 67, 69, 74, 77, 87, 88, 104, 105, 107
Meditation xiii, 110, 131
    Meditation, guided 131
Mindfulness 131
Mindset 36, 70, 91, 109
Mission 9
Mistakes xi, 26, 35, 53, 55, 75, 89, 92, 105, 108
Money 20, 21, 22, 23, 67, 72, 73, 77, 81, 85, 86, 88, 113, 128, 134, 141, 143
Musk, Elon 85

N

Negotiations 36, 87, 88, 89, 90, 91, 143
Networking 36, 128
Neuroscience 41, 129, 142

P

Path vii, xiii, 10, 16, 20, 25, 26, 33, 35, 40, 43, 105, 123, 124, 140

Peace of mind 25, 36, 127
Perfectionism 6
Personal branding 53, 70, 92, 108
Pleasure 42, 50, 113, 126
Positioning 7, 20, 35, 42, 53, 54, 55, 56, 57, 61, 62, 70, 72, 75, 90, 92, 94, 95, 108
Positioning strategy 42, 53, 54, 56, 57, 72
    Positioning strategy Self-Appraisal 61, 62
    Positioning strategy, success factors 48, 54
Positive experiences 131
Positive Thinking 130
Potential xv, 5, 6, 9, 15, 26, 35, 42, 44, 47, 63, 64, 74, 75, 87, 89, 94, 95, 107, 110, 112, 126

R

Relationships 17, 18, 21, 86, 115, 125, 133, 135
    perverse 134, 135
    toxic 18, 22, 28, 36, 76, 133
Research 22, 43, 49, 109, 128, 142
Results v, vi, xiii, 6, 7, 8, 9, 17, 26, 39, 40, 41, 42, 44, 46, 48, 53, 55, 56, 63, 64, 65, 66, 67, 68, 71, 72, 73, 78, 79, 88, 89, 90, 92, 95, 105, 107, 108, 128, 138
Résumé 35, 42, 54, 56, 69, 70, 71, 72, 74, 75

S

Salary 8, 20, 23, 36, 72, 85, 86, 87, 88, 89, 91, 92, 123, 143
    Salary, compensation 88, 89, 123

Salary negotiations 87, 88, 89, 143
    Salary negotiations, pitfalls 70, 74, 89
    Salary negotiations, risks 16, 78, 79, 80, 88, 90, 94, 95, 115
Schmidt, Eric 107
Security 137, 140
Self-appraisal 61, 62
Self-Realization Fellowship 10, 112, 131, 143
Silence 27, 94
Skills vi, 21, 39, 40, 41, 44, 56, 64, 68, 70, 71, 88, 91, 92, 108
Social media 69, 126
Soul 9, 17, 73, 123, 133
Staffing vi, 7, 68
Stakeholders 36, 45, 56
Strengths v, 17, 18, 44, 45, 49, 139, 142
Stress 16, 121, 128, 129
Success v, vi, 17, 20, 25, 40, 41, 47, 48, 49, 54, 71, 74, 92, 107, 108, 109, 111, 125, 127, 128, 129, 139, 141
Synapses 38, 109, 115

T

Talents vi, vii, 5, 7, 9, 26, 35, 40, 41, 42, 43, 44, 45, 46, 47, 48, 49, 50, 51, 52, 55, 56, 65, 66, 69, 70, 71, 76, 77, 78, 79, 80, 94, 96, 104, 124, 125, 126, 139, 142
    Talents, signature talents 35, 40, 41, 43, 44, 49, 65, 96

talktoyardena@careerenlightenacademy.com 5, 63, 136
Thankful 131, 135
Thoughts 15, 17, 20, 22, 36, 38, 42, 44, 45, 49, 89, 102, 110, 112, 115, 119, 121, 124, 128, 130
Transform 18, 61, 79, 101, 112, 114, 115, 121, 126
Trust 78, 136

V

Violence 134, 142
    Violence-free zone 131
Visualizing 40, 101

W

Weaknesses 43
Wellness 126
WhatsApp 63
Working addiction 16
World Economic Forum 108, 143
Worry 9, 16, 19, 48, 67, 72, 78, 85, 103, 140
www.careerenlightenacademy.com 5, 22, 52, 62, 66, 108
www.happinesspathways.com 50, 63, 136

Y

Yoga xiii, 10, 131
Yogananda, Paramahansa 10, 123, 131, 143

www.ingramcontent.com/pod-product-compliance
Lightning Source LLC
Chambersburg PA
CBHW020421220526
45464CB00002B/516